CONSEQUENTIAL LEADERSHIP

15 LEADERS FIGHTING FOR OUR CITIES,

OUR POOR, OUR YOUTH AND OUR CULTURE

Mac Pier

Foreword by **Bob Buford**

Afterword by **Kevin Palau**

IVP Books

An imprint of InterVarsity Press
Downers Grove, Illinois

InterVarsity Press
P.O. Box 1400, Downers Grove, IL 60515-1426
World Wide Web: www.ivpress.com
E-mail: email@ivpress.com

InterVarsity Press® is the book-publishing division of InterVarsity Christian Fellowship/USA®, a
movement of students and faculty active on campus at hundreds of universities, colleges and schools
of nursing in the United States of America, and a member movement of the International Fellowship
of Evangelical Students. For information about local and regional activities, write Public Relations
Dept., InterVarsity Christian Fellowship/USA, 6400 Schroeder Rd., P.O. Box 7895, Madison, WI
53707-7895, or visit the IVCF website at <www.intervarsity.org>.

All Scripture quotations, unless otherwise indicated, are taken from the THE HOLY BIBLE, NEW
INTERNATIONAL VERSION®, NIV® Copyright © 1973, 1978, 1984, 2011 by Biblica, Inc.™ Used
by permission. All rights reserved worldwide.

While all stories in this book are true, some names and identifying information in this book have
been changed to protect the privacy of the individuals involved.

Every effort has been made to trace and contact copyright holders for additional material used in
this book. The authors will be pleased to rectify any omissions in future editions if notified by
copyright holders.

Cover design: Cindy Kiple
Images: City skyline: © Shane Obrien/iStockphoto
        Manhattan cityscape: © bravobravo/iStockphoto
Interior design: Beth Hagenberg

ISBN 978-0-8308-3792-2

Printed in the United States of America ∞

Library of Congress Cataloging-in-Publication Data has been requested.

P   18   17   16   15   14   13   12   11   10   9   8   7   6   5   4   3   2   1

Y   27   26   25   24   23   22   21   20   19   18   17   16   15   14   13   12

"In *Consequential Leadership,* Mac Pier has done us a great service by bringing forth the stories of great entrepreneurs who have crossed over from politics, business and other fields to form a vanguard that may yet bring us back from what the ever-wise David Brooks calls 'a crisis of legitimacy.' These tales are a call to action for all of us."
From the foreword by **Bob Buford**, author of *Halftime*

"Mac Pier clearly demonstrates in this book the importance and impact of God-inspired leadership, which is desperately needed in my part of the world—Sweden, Scandinavia and throughout Europe."
Tomas Brunegård, CEO, Stampen Group; chairman, Swedish Newspaper Publishers' Association; first vice president, World Association of Newspapers and News Publishers

"I appreciate Mac and his diligent quest to understand New York City and help the church there communicate the gospel in a relevant way. He has a long history of promoting widespread prayer for N.Y.C. He is a key influence in advancing the kingdom in cities."
Steve Douglass, president, CRU

"*Consequential Leadership* is an important read for leaders who want to make a world-changing difference for God. The leaders in the book and their stories have literally changed the trajectory of communities, cities and nations."
Dr. Floyd Flake, senior pastor, The Greater Allen AME Cathedral of New York

"*Consequential Leadership* forces us to look inward to find the strength to lead courageously. It moves us to look outward on the plight of society and act with biblical compassion. And it inspires us to look upward in prayer for God's empowering presence. Mac Pier has done it again!"
David D. Ireland, author of *The Skin You Live In*

"I sense that we are in urgent times where leaders must steward their God-given passion to impact the world. Mac Pier has articulated examples of stewards impacting their world."
Raymond H. Harris, RHA Architects, Dallas

"This book is a study of what has already taken place through several consequential leaders, but it is also a challenge to every Christ-follower to continue and multiply that work."
From the afterword by **Kevin Palau**, president, Luis Palau Association

"Leadership matters. The leaders in this book have made an extraordinary difference in their churches, communities and cities. I applaud their impact and invite you to read this book and discover your own leadership assignment."
Rev. Bill Hybels, Chairman & Founder, Willow Creek Association

"The God-stories contained in these biographical sketches will encourage you to see and embrace the God-story of your life."
D. G. Elmore, Chairman, Board of Directors, The Navigators; Chairman, Elmore Companies, Inc.

"Great leaders are as interested in significance as they are in success. In *Consequential Leadership,* Mac Pier profiles fifteen leaders we all want to emulate—great names including W. Wilson Goode Sr., Frances Hesselbein, Luis Palau and Richard Stearns. All are servant leaders whose lives are committed to giving back, locally as well as globally. They are activists, preachers and CEOs. They have created foundations, planted churches, furthered the cause of peace and improved the lives of thousands of people. Read this book—it will inspire you to open your world and become a leader of consequence."
Ken Blanchard, coauthor of *The One Minute Manager*® and *Great Leaders Grow*

Contents

Foreword

The spirit of enterprise is America's greatest asset and its greatest export. This is as true for America's growing churches, nonprofit organizations and government as it is for business. Right now, however, this spirit is deeply imperiled. We are in the worst fix since the Depression and the two World Wars. And it is not a problem of short duration or easy solution.

In the opinion of the late Peter Drucker, "What we have in the developed world is not so much an economic problem as it is a moral problem." The authors of a recent book on Drucker's life pick up on this as well: while others stressed technique and skills, "the human component was most important to Peter Drucker," they write. "This was in large part because of the strong Judeo-Christian underpinnings to Drucker's overall concept of management as a way to achieve a *moral* society comprised of institutions. For Drucker, management was a moral force, not merely a tool at the service of the amoral market."[1]

New York Times columnist David Brooks also stressed the moral aspect in his op-ed titled "The Spirit of Enterprise":

> Why are nations like Germany and the U.S. rich? It's not primarily because they possess natural resources—many nations have those. *It's primarily because of habits, values and social capital.*

It's because many people in these countries, as Arthur Brooks of the American Enterprise Institute has noted, believe in a simple moral formula: effort should lead to reward as often as possible.

This crisis of legitimacy is unlikely to be solved by business or politics-as-usual. It is not a problem that is amenable to money or power. What we need is a moral renaissance rooted in the intersection of faith and action—action that grows out of character, commitment and values.

There *is* hope, but not of the sort that dominates the headlines that thrive on conflict and controversy. Rather, there's hope from organizations like Halftime, which is helping a generation of heroic, highly skilled activists devote the second half of their lives to encore careers of meaning and significance—meaning and significance that come only from following God's call to selfless service.

There's hope from people like Rich Stearns (see chapter six), who left the commercial world as CEO of Lennox China to serve the poor. Through Stearns's superb leadership skills, he took World Vision from $350 million dollars to $1.2 billion in annual revenue.

Wilson Goode, the first African American mayor of Philadelphia, is also spreading hope (see chapter nine). As former mayor of Philadelphia he had thirty thousand employees and a budget of two billion dollars. He himself went from church to church to church recruiting mentors for the children of men in prison. I still carry a business card Wilson gave me when I interviewed him for my book *Finishing Well*. One side of the card states the mission of his organization, Amachi: "people of faith mentoring children of promise." On the reverse side of the card, in Wilson's own handwriting, is one of the clearest business plans I have ever seen (see figure 0.1).

Amachi has already served at least three hundred thousand children.

Hope is also springing from Frances Hesselbein, former president of Girl Scouts of America (see chapter eight). She and I have been what Frances calls "partners for life" since we cofounded, with Richard Schubert, the Peter F. Drucker Foundation for Nonprofit Management, now the Frances Hesselbein Leadership Institute, thirty years ago. Frances says, "I have a very strong belief that we are called

Figure 0.1.

to do what we do, and when we are called we are given the energy."

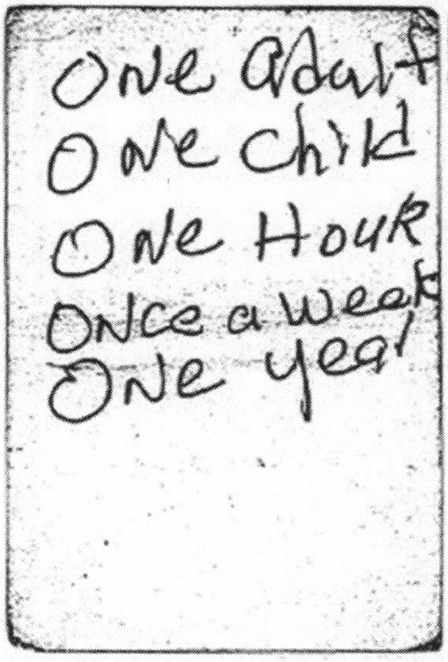

Jim Mellado (see chapter fourteen) is yet another example of hope, and one of the stars of the work of the Leadership Network, an organization for which I serve as chairman, whose focus is applying Peter Drucker's principles to the exponential growth of evangelical churches in the United States. As both an athlete who qualified for the Olympics and a graduate of Harvard Business School, he is one of the smartest people I know and clearly could have made millions. Instead, Jim chose to build the Willow Creek Association, which has provided leadership training for thousands of churches across the globe that have experienced significant growth. In the United States alone, churches with one thousand attendees in a normal weekend have grown in number from one hundred when Willow Creek and the Leadership Network were just beginning to over seven thousand today. Tim Keller, of Redeemer Presbyterian in New York City, has a similar story (see chapter two). Keller left the academic world to begin Redeemer and is now planting churches in cosmopolitan cities across the globe. And, as Peter Drucker was quoted in *Forbes* as saying, "The pastoral megachurches that have been growing so very fast in the U.S. since 1980 . . . are surely the most important social phenomenon in American society in the last 30 years."[2]

In *Consequential Leadership*, Mac Pier has done us a great service by bringing forth the stories of great entrepreneurs who have crossed over from politics, business and other fields to form a vanguard that may yet bring us back from what the ever-wise David Brooks calls "a crisis of legitimacy." These tales are a call to action for all of us.

BOB BUFORD
Founding Chairman, Leadership Network/Halftime
Author, *Halftime* and *Finishing Well*

In Appreciation

I want to thank my family for being on the journey together—Marya, Anna, Jordan and Kirsten, who have given me the freedom for thirty years to travel, experiment and write about big ideas.

I want to thank my team—Lauren, Tom, Beverly, Gary, Carlos, Dee Ann, Sharon, Stephanie, Ken, Pam, Ebony, Ramona, Caren, Annette and Natisha—for their shared sacrifice for the vision of a changed New York City.

I want to thank Julie Ackerman Link for her brilliant work in editing this book. She has become a great friend and colleague.

I want to thank Andy Le Peau and the team at InterVarsity Press for believing in this simple effort to describe what is possible through ordinary lives possessed by extraordinary passion.

Special thanks to Beverly Cook for her efforts to finalize the manuscript.

I want to thank all of the leaders in this book who generously gave their time to transparently share their journeys with me and with the world.

DEDICATION

I dedicate this book to a growing community of colleagues fighting for the welfare of their communities and cities—often in anonymity and decades of effort. Thanks for being on the journey together.

Atlanta—Chip Sweney

Boston—Doug and Judy Hall, Jeff Bass, Bobby Bose

Chicago—Phil Miglioratti, Scott Chapman

Corvallis—Tom White

Dallas—Rebecca Walls, Mario Zandstra, Jim Runyan, Jeff Warren, Brian Considine, Ed Pearce, Raymond Harris, Marydel Harris and Doug Kramp

Denver—Dave Runyon

Houston—Jim Herrington and Steve Capper

Jackson—Jarvis Ward

Minneapolis—Glenn Barth

New York—Mark Reynolds, Scott Kauffmann, Chris Troy, Paul Coty, Jeremy Del Rio, Matt Bennett

Phoenix—Gary Kinnaman, Billy Thrall

Portland—Kevin Palau, Ben Sands

San Diego—Mike Carlisle, Sam Williams

1

Introduction

CONSEQUENTIAL TIMES

*The most exalted idea applied to God
is not infinite wisdom, infinite power,
but infinite concern.*

Abraham Heschel, *The Prophets*

On September 11, 2001, I was sitting on the fifteenth floor of the Empire State Building preparing for the annual board meeting of Concerts of Prayer Greater New York when board member Tom Mahairas stuck his head in the door at 8:50 a.m. He had just gotten a phone call from his daughter, who said that a plane had crashed into a tower of the World Trade Center and that people were jumping out the windows of the one hundredth floor. We assumed that the pilot of a small plane had accidentally flown into the building. Thirty minutes later we got news of the second attack. Within minutes we were sitting in the tallest building in New York City. We scrambled down to Fifth Avenue, two miles north of the World Trade Center. Smoke and dust billowed across the avenue. Thousands of dazed and disoriented New Yorkers wandered the streets.

My children had gone to school that morning with one parent in Manhattan and another in Washington, D.C., where my wife, Marya, was attending a cardiology conference with Dr. William

Tenet, the twin brother of CIA director George Tenet. Phone service was unavailable for several hours, so none of us knew whether or not other family members were alive. For a time, Marya thought she might be spending the night at George's home. I was able to get home that night because I had driven into Manhattan (which was unusual for me to do). But even there, in the weeks ahead, the schools my two older children attended received bomb threats. Terrorism hit very close to home.

September 11 became a defining moment in U.S. history. No other single day saw as much death on U.S. soil—three thousand lives were lost. Some were eviscerated by the explosion. Some leapt to their deaths to escape the flames. Claudia Roux, a colleague with Alpha, and her coworkers couldn't return to their downtown offices for weeks due to bio dust from human remains. Weeks later, cars parked below ground level in the World Trade Center were still smoldering at one thousand degrees.

The paradox of September 11 is the number of Americans who were spared. The courageous work of the New York City Fire Department, the New York City Police Department and the Metropolitan Transportation Authority saved thousands of lives. Men and women ran into burning, collapsing buildings to rescue as many people as possible. One woman being escorted out of a building asked a fireman why he was going inside. The fireman responded simply, "This is what I do." Courage made the difference.

In addition, for many weeks emergency workers and volunteers scoured the remains of buildings at Ground Zero hoping to find one more lost loved one. Nonprofit leaders and agencies sprang into action providing food, relief and resources to victims. On September 13, I was sitting in the parking lot of a Connecticut diner when I received a phone call from World Vision asking if Concerts of Prayer Greater New York would cocreate a relief fund for the victims. Together we started the American Families Assistance Fund; by the end of 2011, we had raised six million dollars, which was distributed to victims of 9/11 largely through the efforts of New York City churches.

Churches were actively involved from the day of the attacks. One Chinatown church, Oversea Chinese Mission, for example, fed five hundred people every day for months. Primitive Christian Church, under the leadership of pastor Marc Rivera, provided round-the-clock assistance to people who needed rest, food and counseling. Pastor Rivera said, "If the Twin Towers had tipped rather than imploded straight down, they would have reached all the way to the doorstep of my church." The follow-up initiatives in the church community after September 11 awakened a desire to revive New York City. Leaders came to plant churches, start careers and give themselves to serve a city that was broken.

On a personal level, September 11 left me with three life-changing impressions. First was the immediacy of eternity. Three thousand people went to work that day with no idea that they would not return home. In the time it takes a heart to beat, they went from an ordinary day in the office to the door of eternity. Cantor Fitzgerald, whose offices were on floors 101 to 105 of the World Trade Center, lost more than six hundred employees. When CEO Howard Lutnick participated in a memorial service one month later at the Christian Cultural Center in Brooklyn, he spoke about the devastation of the attack and confessed that he had no idea how to rebuild his life or his company.

Second, I was struck by the power of agreement. Nineteen terrorists changed the world by agreeing with their superiors to commandeer airplanes and fly them into the greatest symbols of American democracy and capitalism. Now, no one travels by plane or takes a ride into Manhattan without thinking about September 11. Rebuilding the economy is taking years, and it is likely that our sense of national security will never be restored.

Third, I saw the importance of global cities. New York City wasn't a random choice. It was chosen specifically because an

MY STORY
Consequential Times, Catalytic Events, Christlike Mentors

Standing in the bleachers at the Urbana Student Missions Conference on December 30, 1979, with my beloved Marya, whom I would marry one year later, was an unforgettable experience. For three days we had been listening to John Stott's heart-gripping exposition of Romans. Now Billy Graham was challenging us to go anywhere in the world God called us. Marya and I stood to say yes to God.

Since that night God has used various mentors and catalytic events to guide us to New York City:

- *David Bryant's writing and speaking provided for me a global worldview and a deepening understanding of the supremacy of Christ.*

- *Ray Bakke's teaching on the centrality of cities in fifteen years of urban consultations and doctoral courses involved showing, not just telling. During a fifteen-year period he took me on trips to Johannesburg, Manila and Vancouver and on many excursions in New York City.*

- *John Clause from World Vision opened my eyes to the world of the HIV pandemic. As a result I have taken ten trips to East Africa.*

- *Bill Hybels and his Willow Creek Association team introduced me to the centrality of leadership in effecting measurable change in difficult contexts from a biblical perspective, and the idea that "leaders do what leadership requires." That concept was the seed of the New York City Leadership Center. I founded the New York City Leadership Center along with my staff team and board in 2007. After twenty years of journeying with New York City pastors and mission leaders, we saw the urgent need to provide training resources and collaborative opportunities to transform our city.*

- *The pastoral community of New York City (Bob Johansson, Roderick Caesar, Ron Bailey, Luciano Padilla) and scores of other leaders immersed me in the beauty and challenges of local church life in the inner city.*
- *A 1983 trip to India taught me the power of extended, united, corporate prayer as I gathered with other believers every Friday for three to nine hours of prayer.*
- *Selling our possessions to move to New York City in 1984 was the most radical faith step we have taken, but God transcended our risk with his provision.*

Three spheres—campus, city and church—form the crucible in which I have attempted to become more Christlike. I served for seventeen years with InterVarsity on campus as a student leader and staff member. I was shaped by the godly supervision of Clayton Lindgren, Janet Luhrs Balajthy and Bobby Gross. I was deeply impacted by the Bible teaching of Barbara Boyd and the Urbana Student Missions Conferences. The promise of Psalm 23:3 has proven true: God *has* guided me into paths of righteousness for his name's sake.

---

attack on the media and financial center of the world was a way of attacking the entire Western world.

In his book *Perspectives on the World Christian Movement*, Ralph Winter suggests that every four hundred years a global event radically changes the trajectory of the church. Beginning with the crucifixion (A.D. 33), followed by the invasion of the Barbarians of Rome (A.D. 410), the invasion of the Vikings and the capture of Dublin (A.D. 834), the Crusades (A.D. 1095-1291), the missionary work of William Carey to the Indian coast (A.D. 1793) and Hudson Taylor to inland China (A.D. 1853), each four-hundred-year epoch represents the geographic progression of the gospel. Winter surmises that God grew the church during each period, dark as some of them were.[1]

Is it possible that September 11 marked the beginning of one of those four-hundred-year periods? Only history will tell. But a cosmic conflict between Western culture and an ideology of terror rooted in religious extremism does not seem coincidental.

This book is about leading consequentially. A consequential leader fully enters with their spiritual community into the concerns of God and the suffering of Christ for the world. Consequential leaders act to address the greatest spiritual, social and humanitarian concerns on the heart of God. This book is about those kinds of leaders and helping us to aspire toward being more consequential in our leadership.

CONSEQUENTIAL REALITIES

There are three demographics today that represent a majority, or near majority, of the world's population: people living in metropolitan areas (urban), people under twenty-five years of age (young) and people living on less than two dollars a day (poor). Consequential times require leaders who can address these major demographic groups.

Global cities. In 2002, Ray Bakke, retired chancellor of Bakke Graduate University, wrote:

> The astonishing new fact of our time is that the majority of the world's six billion people now live and work in sizeable cities. Moreover, we live at the time of the greatest migration in human history. The southern hemisphere is moving north, East is coming West, and everyone is coming to New York! I remember well the day several years ago when, sitting in Manhattan, I read a *New York Times* report that 133 nations had been found living together in one Queens zip code.[2]

Bakke describes the trend in American cities, in particular: "In the first hundred years after colonization people moved west to farms. In the second hundred years people moved north to cities. Now in the third century we are seeing the internationalization of American cities with people from all over the globe."[3] The U.S. now has the largest Jewish population, with more Jews than Tel Aviv. It also has more Spanish speakers than Spain, the largest Irish population and one of the largest Scandinavian populations in the world. These immigrant communities are concentrated in many U.S. cities and New York City in particular. In one decade, more than one million immigrants moved into New York City. New York City is the largest Jewish city outside Israel and one of the largest Muslim cities outside the Islamic world.

However, though the U.S. has a high concentration of immigrants, other countries have many more highly populated cities than it does. Of the five hundred cities with a population of more than one million people, the majority are in Asia, Africa and Latin America. China, for example, is experiencing an annual influx of more than sixteen million people—roughly the population of Canada—into its cities from rural areas. It is not a coincidence, then, that the rapid growth of Christianity corresponds to the rapid growth of cities on those three continents. The rapid growth of Christianity is happening right now. Between 1900 and 2050, the percentage of Christians globally from Africa, Asia and Latin America is forecast to grow from 22 percent to 71 percent, according to Bob Doll in his Lausanne 2010 seminar at Cape Town, South Africa. China has the fastest-growing church in the world, according to Ray Bakke in a 2008 lecture at Faith Bible College in Flushing, New York.

The posture of the United States toward the world has changed. With the opening of Ellis Island in 1891 the United States faced east to Europe, allowing in people of Protestant, Catholic and Jewish faith. Today the country faces west toward Asia, as 60 percent of the world lives in the Pacific Rim. Together, India and China contain 40 percent of the world's population. In his same seminar at Cape Town, Bob Doll noted that China has the fastest-growing economy. Tom Friedman has stated that India has the fastest-growing middle class in the world. No longer are neighbors in U.S. cities from only the faith traditions of Abraham (Judaism, Christianity and Islam). Eastern religions, including Buddhism and Hinduism (also New Age), along with aggressive secularism and atheism, are competing for attention.[4]

This great global reality represents an unprecedented opportunity for communities long separated from the truth of God in Christ to encounter the gospel. After moving to New York City in 1984, I met a jewelry dealer on an airplane whose daughter was the same age as my youngest daughter. The jewelry dealer was a Sikh from the Punjab of India and was married to a Hindu. We became friends and visited each other's homes. When my friend's mother became ill and slipped into a coma we prayed for her and she was miraculously healed. This provided the opportunity to talk about the God to whom we pray. God was setting up this opportunity to reveal himself to a family who had no significant contact with the gospel. God is choreographing global neighbors into our urban U.S. neighborhoods to fulfill his purposes; we need to seize the opportunities all around us.

The young. In the spring of 2011 the world witnessed the outrage of young people across the Arab world, with the unrest spreading through the Middle East at the speed of social networking. The "Arab Spring" demonstrated what happens when oppressive governments make young people feel so hopeless that they are willing to risk their lives for a taste of freedom.

Many young people in urban centers are profoundly challenged. In the United States, crime has exploded. Twenty-five percent of the global prison population is in our country; on any given day more than seven million people are in the penal system in America.[5] We have become a capital of incarceration. The state of New York alone has more than eighty-five thousand inmates[6]; of those, Ray Bakke estimates that 80 percent come from six zip codes.

Gary Frost, president of Concerts of Prayer Greater New York, was the highest-ranking minority leader with the North American Missions Board prior to his move to New York City. As part of his ministry now, he regularly visits young African American and Hispanic men in prison. Prison visitation is disheartening, he admits, but having to conduct funerals is even worse. "I have conducted too many funerals over the lives of young African American men killed senselessly," Frost says. "To hear the sobbing and the wrenching of mothers who have lost their children is unbearable." He recounts a specific experience he had: "I was walking one day with my son Timothy through the cemetery of Youngstown, Ohio, and my son counted forty tombstones of his friends. He could not take it anymore so he just stopped counting."[7] Frost and his wife, Lynette, have worked to alleviate the crisis by serving as foster parents to forty children.

Young people in large cities are also vulnerable academically. In a January 2009 interview by Bob Costas, Tony Dungy, former head coach of the Indianapolis Colts, was asked by Costas whether he would return to coaching. Dungy responded, "I will probably not return to coach. The most significant reason for not returning is to address the needs of young people. In Indianapolis we only have a 19 percent graduation rate."[8] Other estimates indicate that the graduation rate in Indianapolis may be as high as 30 percent, but it is still the second lowest in the nation; only Detroit is lower.[9]

The reality is that in many of our urban centers across the country, a near majority of young people are not graduating from high school. This is creating a social time bomb. Frances Hesselbein, CEO of the Girl Scouts for thirteen years, says that unless something dramatic is done, this trend will undermine democracy. Young people without hope will protest.

Another form of hopelessness that grips young people is secularism. In 1998 David Sue, staff member with Concerts of Prayer Greater New York, surveyed the diverse religious community of

Flushing, New York, speaking with Muslims, Jews, Buddhists, Hindus and Christians. He found one common thread—everyone was losing faith in the religious tradition of their ancestors. Secularism was drawing young people away from their ancestral beliefs. The percentage of young people who discontinue their involvement in church upon graduation from college is as high as 90 percent.[10]

Pastor Anthony Trufant of Emmanuel Baptist Church in Brooklyn is working to address this. He has a successful three-part strategy for reaching young people in his church, helping them become multilingual, crosscultural and technologically literate. Trufant implemented programs along these lines when he started the church, which has grown to several hundred members.

The doors are wide open for churches to make an incredible, relevant difference in the lives of young people. Intersecting with young people where they have expressed interests is urgently important.

The poor. Ron Sider's 1978 book *Rich Christians in an Age of Hunger* and Rich Stearns's 2009 book *The Hole in Our Gospel* have become bookends on the subject of poverty. Troubled by the stark contrast between wealth in America (U.S. citizens living in the middle class enjoy being in the ninety-ninth percentile of global wealth) and poverty across the globe, these two men have challenged American Christians to recognize their responsibility to the poor.

Much of the population in east and southern Africa, devastated for thirty years by HIV and AIDS, lives on less than one dollar a day. In the developing world, most people live on less than two dollars a day; Haitians—in our own hemisphere—also live on less than two dollars a day. When I traveled to Port-au-Prince in March 2010, ten weeks after the earthquake of January 12, the landscape looked many times worse than New York City after the September 11 attacks. The entire city—not just two skyscrapers—had crumbled into rubble. Clean water and sanitation were nearly impossible to find. More than one million Haitians lived in makeshift tents. According to one estimate, it will take three hundred years to clear all of the debris at the current rate of rubble removal.

Thankfully, as in the aftermath of September 11, Christians are responding. A coalition of agencies has agreed to a goal of creating one hundred thousand new jobs in Haiti by the tenth anniversary of the earthquake. According to Doug Seebeck, president of Partners Worldwide, that many new jobs would double the economy in the country.[11]

There is a need for a huge army of marketplace leaders to provide skill training for ever-emerging talent in the Two-Thirds World.

A NEED FOR HEROES

As I interviewed leaders for this book, two patterns emerged. Nearly all of them were influenced by (1) extraordinary mentors and (2) catalytic events. I consistently heard about the influence of Billy Graham, John Stott, Ray Bakke and John Perkins. I also heard consistently about events like Lausanne and Urbana. Moreover, it became clear that the richest source of vision for this leadership community has been Scripture. On page after page of the Bible we meet leaders who rose to the challenge of consequential times, leading a nation out of slavery, fending off starvation or intervening to prevent genocide.

One of the most consequential times in the Old Testament happened in the fifth century B.C. during the reign of Xerxes, king of Persia. At that time Persia was divided into 127 provinces extending from Ethiopia to India. Chronicling events that took place in what is now Iran, the Old Testament books of Ezra, Nehemiah and Esther form a "Persian Trilogy" and create a paradigm on how to lead consequentially. Ezra led God's people to renewal by pointing them back to the Scriptures. Nehemiah mobilized the laity to rebuild Jerusalem. Esther used her position as queen to change the law and save her people.

Esther was raised by her cousin Mordecai after she became an orphan. When King Xerxes was looking for a new queen after deposing the previous one, Esther won his favor and was selected to fill the role. The orphan became a queen. While she was queen, the highest-ranking noble in the king's inner circle hatched a plot to destroy Mordecai and all the Jews.

When Mordecai learned of the plot, he tore his clothes and went into the city wailing loudly and bitterly. He understood the consequential times in which he was living and could not accept the incongruity between the promises of God for the Jewish people and the law authorizing their annihilation. Mordecai therefore appealed to his cousin Esther to intervene on behalf of the Jewish people. His response serves as a model for us of the appropriate reaction to a horrific reality—a reality that many in the world face today: he entered the reality of their danger. We must do the same.

The response of those of us in the West, however, is often like Esther's initial response. She denied the seriousness of the situation and sent Mordecai a set of new clothes, urging him to change out of his mourning attire. Like her, we simply give to meet superficial needs. Doing so helps us compensate for our own sense of meaninglessness, but it does nothing to bring meaning to those in danger of losing their lives. Esther also responded in fear, stating that her life would be in jeopardy if she approached the king without being invited. We do the same when we fail to take risks because we are more concerned about the longevity of our lives than about the needs of people or the purposes of God.

Mordecai demonstrated leadership by defining reality and making Esther's choice clear to her. She could stand up for her people, recognizing that God had placed her in a unique position at a unique moment to make a dynamic difference, or she could cower in a corner and watch God use someone else. Esther decided to become consequential, agreeing to approach the king on behalf of her people even though it could cost her her life.

What happened? The crucial element in Esther's story is her appeal to other Jews. She invited them to fast with her for three days, taking no water or food. By standing with her in spiritual agreement, her Jewish community gave her the strength to risk everything, to be consequential. Indeed, in the past two thousand years of church history, the common thread of the great spiritual movements beginning in the early church—the German Moravians who prayed for twenty-four hours a day and sent out missionaries, the British Clapham Sect who prayed three hours a day and worked to get legislation passed that freed slaves from the British Empire, and the Franciscans who changed Europe—is this: they all practiced corporate spiritual disciplines. A spiritual community is crucial for consequential leadership.

Given the enormity of need in the world today, there has never been a more important time to live consequentially. The story of Esther, Mordecai and the Jewish community demonstrates the starting point. Be a mentor and find a mentor. Be part of a community that exercises both personal and corporate spiritual disciplines. Pay attention to your life and listen to God so you can understand his call to you in your context. And let the leaders in this book be "authorial mentors" for your own consequential leadership. They are our "great cloud of witnesses" and have contributed to changing the spiritual, social and humanitarian landscape of the planet.

It seemed fitting for September 11, 2011, to fall on a Sunday, since God and his people provide the appropriate context for finding the meaning of salvation, world history and our unique participation in the great eternal drama. My prayer for us is that we hear the whispers of God and become increasingly like his Son, who became flesh and dwelt among us, providing for us the most consequential possibility of all—eternal life that starts now in sacrifice with and for others.

This is my prayer for us.

Jesus,

We thank you that you lived your life consequentially. We thank you that you came in the fullness of time as a first-century Jew in the Roman Empire. In your birth, you identified with all of humanity as an Asian-born baby who became an African refugee. In your work, you identified with the common laborer as a carpenter's son. In your social life, you identified with all of the single people by remaining unmarried. In your death, you identified with the abused and slaughtered. In your burial, you identified with the homeless by being placed in a borrowed tomb. And in your triumphant resurrection, the most consequential moment of all history, you rescue all of us by proving your power over death and guaranteeing our eternal life. Help us to understand the uniqueness of being made in the image of God, and to understand our unique assignment to represent you in our communities. May our lives and our leadership draw us into greater conformity to you—and may we live consequentially.

Tim Keller

The Story of a New York City Church-Planting Movement

LEARN: Do with your life what will have the most impact. Founding a grace-centered, gospel-centric church-planting movement in New York City was a world-changing choice.

SUCCEED: Understand the compelling message of God's grace and how it can attract anyone, even in the hardest places.

Tim Keller is a rare gift—to me, to New York City and to city movements around the globe.

For the past twenty-five years he has been both a personal mentor and a partner in ministry. He and I both believe that New York City is on the precipice of a faith-filled century not seen for several generations.

In 1987, Keller was spending time in New York City, and I was on staff with InterVarsity Christian Fellowship in the city. He called me to find out about existing ministry networks. Soon after that initial phone call we had our first meeting.

The longer I work with Keller, the more I appreciate him. His deep faith, humility, intellectual prowess and grand efforts to reach people make his life remarkable. His faith is expressed in a robust prayer life, and his humility in a great desire to work with others. His intellectual prowess is demonstrated by the quality of his thought and the volume of his content. His grand efforts to reach people are rooted in a vision for a global city church-planting movement starting in New York City.

DEFINING MOMENTS

Tim Keller was born in 1950 and raised in Lehigh Valley, Pennsylvania. Growing up he attended a mainline church with his family. Although he participated in confirmation classes, he never experienced conversion to Christ. "When I entered Bucknell University, I did my best to avoid groups like InterVarsity," Keller says, "but a friend in my dorm finally convinced me to attend. Through the ministry of InterVarsity, I was challenged to read the Bible and to weigh its claims on my life."[1]

In his book *King's Cross*, Keller writes about his conversion: "Though as a youth I had believed that the Bible was the Word of the Lord, I had not personally met the Lord of the Word. As I read the Gospels, he became real to me. Thirty years later I preached through the book of Mark at my church in New York City, in the hope that many others would likewise find Jesus in the accounts of the Gospels."[2]

In the early years of his faith, Keller was influenced by the writings of C. S. Lewis, John Stott and J. I. Packer. These British thinkers, theologians and writers had the intellectual substance to define Christianity as a credible belief system. Having become a Christian in a university setting, Keller appreciated the need for an intellectually rigorous faith. This would be crucial to his emergence as a thought leader in Manhattan, where a high percentage of people are skeptics. Keller says the majority of New Yorkers, rooted in secularism, consider belief in a supernatural God to be strange and out of touch with reality.[3]

After college, Keller enrolled in Gordon-Conwell Theological Seminary in Boston, where he completed a Master of Divinity in 1975. Sensing the call to pastoral ministry, Keller became pastor of a small church in Virginia, where he served for nine years. During this time he also taught as an adjunct professor at Westminster Seminary.

When Tim met Terry Gyger in the 1980s, he didn't realize that it would be a life-changing encounter. Gyger was a member of the national leadership team of the Presbyterian Church of America (PCA), and his assignment was to oversee the planting of new churches. "Gyger had a vision to plant a flagship church in Manhattan that would in turn plant other congregations," said Keller. "But previous attempts to plant such a church had not been successful." Gyger traveled to Manhattan every quarter to lay the groundwork for the eventual church-planting team, and he involved Keller in the research for the new church.

"While I was doing the research, Gyger invited two leaders to plant the church," Keller said. "Both turned him down." Gyger then asked Keller to move to Manhattan. Nothing in Keller's background as the pastor of a modest congregation in Virginia or as professor at Westminster Seminary had prepared him to plant a church in a strongly secular urban setting.

But the obvious answer—no—did not come out of Keller's mouth. Something beyond logic and common sense was at work. In addition to Gyger's encouragement, two other influential voices were resounding in Keller's conscience. Harvie Conn and Richard Greenway, both faculty members in urban ministry at Westminster Seminary, had spoken often with Keller about the importance of cities to influence culture. The combined influence of these men brought Keller to a place of deep conviction that cities are important to God and strategic to the global advancement of the gospel.

Instead of giving the easy answer, Keller gave the answer that demonstrated the depth of his faith. He said yes to Gyger. But more importantly, he said yes to God.

In 1989, Keller and his wife, Kathy, moved their family to New York City to start Redeemer Presbyterian Church.[4] Back then Manhattan had very little Christian influence. "There were very few churches," Keller says. "It has been estimated that there were only about nine thousand evangelical Christians in central Manhattan.

"Since then, through the establishment of nearly one hundred new churches, the faith population has nearly quadrupled to an estimated thirty-four thousand Christians. Redeemer has been the largest influence in establishing these new churches through training and grants to church planters."[5]

Under Keller's leadership, Redeemer established Redeemer City to City (RCTC), a separate not-for-profit agency, to focus on mobilizing church-planting movements in urban centers and to distribute books and training materials.[6]

In 2010 alone, RCTC helped plant churches in Tokyo, Barcelona, Johannesburg, São Paulo, Kuala Lumpur and fifteen other cities for a total of thirty-four. Keller and his team have become one of the most effective urban church-planting agencies in the world.

Keller is considered to be the leading intellectual force behind gospel movements penetrating cities. In a 2006 survey of two thousand church leaders, *Christianity Today* cited Redeemer as the sixteenth most influential church in America.[7]

Keller has also become a *New York Times* bestselling author. Since 2008, he has written *Reason for God, Prodigal God, Counterfeit Gods, Generous Justice* and *Gospel in Life*. Former President George W. Bush references Keller as an influence in his own conversion. In his autobiography, *Decision Points,* Bush quotes from Keller's *Reason for God* when describing the "clues of God" that pointed toward a forgiving God to whom he would commit his life.[8]

CONSEQUENTIAL IMPACT

Every Sunday more than five thousand people worship at one of Redeemer's six services, which are held on the east and west side

BEING "WORLD HISTORICAL"

Through his writing and preaching, John Stott was a mentor to Keller. When asked to speak at Stott's memorial service in the U.S., Keller read six books about his life. "Stott made a decision at the age of sixty to do something he considered to be world historical," Keller said later. "He began to invest intentionally in the efforts of leaders globally." To Keller, this was affirmation that the work of the New York City Movement Project[9] has the potential to be "world historical." Keller added, "If we change New York City and reach a tipping point of 10 percent active Christians in Manhattan, I believe this will happen."[10]

---

of Central Park in Manhattan. From the seed of an idea in 1989, Redeemer has grown to become the most effective urban, church-planting congregation in the world. How did this happen?

Keller states three primary reasons for Redeemer's growth. The first and most important, he says, is prayer. At least five hundred congregations were praying for the establishment of Redeemer in 1989. This represented over one hundred thousand people praying that God would give the congregation a successful start. The Women In Church Association of the PCA made Redeemer their national ministry project and provided a significant financial gift.[11]

In addition to the widespread prayer of the denomination, citywide prayer meetings were ongoing. The Concerts of Prayer movement began in February 1988. By 1989, regular gatherings of pastors and churches were being held in all five boroughs of New York City—Manhattan, Queens, Brooklyn, Staten Island and the Bronx. Churches also were gathering for prayer in New Jersey and Long Island. Within twenty years, two hundred thousand people had participated in the prayer movement. An important theme in these prayer meetings was the establishment of new churches. Sensing the need to create a spiritual climate for accelerated spiritual impact in New York City, congregations began a daily prayer vigil in February 1995. Those who participated believe it is no coincidence that between 1995 and 2000 the NYC murder rate dropped 70 percent.

The involvement of new Christians was the second reason for Redeemer's growth, says Keller. Campus Crusade had attracted forty people who were new followers of Christ. This community brought friends and coworkers to Redeemer, which has provided a great church home for young professionals. Redeemer has been effective in connecting with other agencies throughout the city for mutual benefit. These agencies have provided a great vehicle for outreach and service to Redeemer attendees.

A third reason for the church's initial growth, Keller believes, was flexible preaching. In 1989, less than 1 percent of the New York City population was living and worshiping in Manhattan. "Many residents did not know a single, practicing Christian," says Keller, "and the stereotypes they had were not at all flattering." To combat this negative image, Keller met with twenty to thirty people every week at the Tramway Café underneath the 59th Street Bridge in Manhattan. These New Yorkers helped Keller shape the style of his preaching to reach a secular and often skeptical audience. Keller's preaching has been described as "flypaper to the culture," meaning that it provides intellectual "stickiness" for people who question the reasonableness of faith.[12]

As Keller prayed for wisdom and guidance, immersed himself in Scripture and studied church history, three themes became dominant in his thinking: the centrality of the grace of God in all of life; the strategic nature of cities; and the indispensability of city-focused gospel movements fueled by God's grace and sustained by effective leadership.

The main idea: Grace. "Most people believe that Redeemer has grown because of our commitment to intellectual life and our sophistication. That is not it at all. Our core message is simply the grace of God in the gospel. I integrate into every sermon the grace of God in the person of Jesus. Everything else is ornamental." Keller spoke these words in May 2009 to a group of forty pastors brought together by the New York City Leadership Center to hear him describe the core message of his book *The Prodigal God*.[13]

In the hard, secular soil of Manhattan, Keller's message has taken root. People have responded by the thousands to his simple message: "We are more lost than we could have ever imagined but more loved than we ever dared to hope," Keller said at the May 2009 pastors meeting.

In *The Prodigal God* Keller develops the idea of grace. He describes a God who is the real prodigal, a God who is "recklessly extravagant" toward us in sacrificing his Son on our behalf. The elder brother in the story, the hard hearted and ungracious sibling, symbolizes churches characterized by an unforgiving, judgmental spirit, which keeps them from growing.[14]

The story introduces us to the elder brother who resents the younger brother for scandalously squandering their father's estate. He was equally resentful of their father for welcoming the younger brother home and celebrating his return. Keller asserts that many local churches are filled with "elder brothers" who spend more energy criticizing others inside the church than they do looking for ways to love the unlovable outside the church.

Keller challenges us to become like Jesus, the true elder brother. Rather than resent those who have squandered their lives in destructive choices, he encourages us to seek those far from God, just as Jesus, our true elder brother, sought us.

The central place: Cities. Speaking at the third Lausanne Congress, Cape Town 2010 in South Africa, Keller said that one hundred leading global cities drive 30 percent of the global economy and 100 percent of global innovation. Keller's convictions about church planting are rooted in his understanding of the New Testament. The apostle Paul never traveled to a small city— only cities large enough to influence culture. Reaching cities, Keller believes, is central to reaching the culture for Christ.[15]

As stated in chapter one, more than half of the world's population fits one of three groups: people younger than twenty-five years of age, people living on less than two dollars a day, and people living in cities. Keller and Redeemer City to City focus on global cities because they have a disproportionate influence on the rest of the world. Keller believes that four cities shape the globe more than any others: New York City, London, Tokyo and Paris.

Church planting is the core strategy for reaching cities. Churches that are ten years and younger are six times more effective in reaching new people than churches ten years and older. This conclusion has been borne out by the growth of the Christian population in Manhattan in the past decade. Of the two hundred churches surveyed in 2009, 39 percent had been established since 2001.[16]

Keller and his team at RCTC have articulated an understanding of citywide "gospel ecosystems." Their conviction is that every city has a spiritual environment represented by churches, mission agencies and leaders. "An effective gospel ecosystem," says Keller, "is one in which all of these, working collaboratively, love their cities on behalf of Christ."[17] This results in church growth, penetration of the culture through effective leadership and an increased sense of justice for the city.

The essential element: Gospel movements. A gospel movement takes place when the population of Christians grows faster than the general population. In many cities, the Christian population is small and struggling. When a work of renewal takes place and the Christian population begins to grow, the whole city is affected.

New York City has an important history of gospel movements.

The 1857-1858 Fulton Street Revival ushered in a remarkable sixty-year period of church growth. A prayer meeting that began near Wall Street mushroomed into a daily gathering of fifty thousand New Yorkers with as many as ten thousand conversions recorded weekly. The national population saw one million conversions in two years from a national population of thirty million.

The year 1865 marked the birth of many social concern movements, including the Bowery Mission, the McCauley Street Mission, and Christian and Missionary Alliance. Thousands of poor and destitute people were rescued. The Student Volunteer Movement accelerated in New York City in 1888, motivating twenty-five thousand young people to enlist in foreign missions over the next forty years. One missionary, Horace Underwood, ignited the flame of Christianity in Korea.[18] In the United States, freed slaves were taught literacy by Baptist and Methodist missionaries. The response to the gospel was so strong that by 1900 more African Americans had become Christians than any other ethnic group in North American history.

Under Keller's leadership, Redeemer is helping to fuel a modern-day gospel movement. Keller's teaching has become a magnet, attracting leaders from cities worldwide. In September 2010 and 2011, RCTC and the New York City Leadership Center coled the first two annual Movement Day conferences, an initiative that brought together nearly two thousand leaders from thirty-four cities and fourteen nations. The event offered urban leaders from local churches, ministry agencies and the marketplace an opportunity to share best practices and innovative ways to influence cities. Leaders with expertise in reaching youth, university students and marketplace peers joined those with expertise in planting urban churches. Together they mapped a plan for increasing their influence. As a result, ten cities—Atlanta, Boston, Chicago, Dallas, Denver, Houston, New York City, Phoenix, Portland and San Diego—committed to a five-year journey of peer learning. The Luis Palau Association manages a website—www. gospelmovements.org—that emerged from Movement Day 2010.

Redeemer has spawned several agencies that are affecting the culture of New York City. Hope for New York catalyzes thousands of volunteers and funding to partner with grass-roots service agencies affecting the homeless and destitute in New York City. The Center for Faith and Work disciples marketplace leaders to comprehend their vocational callings. Redeemer City to City trains church planters and provides curriculum for leaders in global cities.

Leading in tough times. The leadership team of Redeemer has not avoided stormy times, and Keller is transparent in describing the four seasons of Redeemer's life.

1989-1993: Good Chaos. The church grew quickly to fifteen hundred attendees with more than one hundred people per year becoming Christians. Keller estimates that between three and five hundred people became Christians during this first season, a time of genuine revival and dynamic church growth that Manhattan had not seen in decades.

1994-2000: Order. Redeemer hired Dick Kaufmann to join the team and build the infrastructure of the church. Kaufmann was a Harvard graduate and church planter. He built the systems for the church and helped to expand the network of small groups. The church grew from fifteen hundred to twenty-eight hundred in regular attendance. Redeemer developed a philosophy that if you weren't in a small group, you weren't really in the church.

2001-2005: Bad Chaos. The trauma of 9/11 dramatically affected the church's finances even as the church continued to grow. The church had more people but less income. Dick Kaufmann had moved on to plant a church in San Diego. Keller was diagnosed with thyroid cancer that required surgery. The combination of financial, leadership and health trauma took its toll on the staff, yet the church grew to thirty-six hundred regular attendees.

2006-2011: Order. God brought to the pastoral team Bruce Terrell, who consolidated Redeemer into stable growth and grew the pastoral team. Terrell prepared to launch Redeemer into a season of decentralization, in which the church would become multiple congregations, each with its own pastoral leadership, rather than one congregation with Keller as its senior pastor. The plan represents a careful succession strategy that will allow Keller to do more speaking and training of leaders in global cities. Church attendance averages more than fifty-four hundred per week.[19]

KELLER'S PLAN TO ESTABLISH A CHRISTIAN PRESENCE IN A MAJOR CITY

1. *Begin with a major prayer effort.*

2. *Set a "tipping point" goal of 10 percent resident Christians.*

3. *Establish resources for a ten-year church-planting effort to lay the groundwork for reaching the 10 percent goal.*

4. *Engage the culture of the city. View culture as a strategy for reaching people, not as an enemy to avoid or overcome.*

5. *Preach a clear, simple message of grace.*

VISION

Keller's vision for the next twenty years is to see the residential Christian population of Manhattan grow to one hundred thousand. He believes that if four hundred new churches can be established in Manhattan, the Christian population will triple. Why is this number important?

"If we grow to become a Christian population of one hundred thousand in Manhattan, or roughly 10 percent of the resident population," says Keller, "we will achieve a tipping point. By then we will have Christians in the places of influence in our city—in academic, media and cultural places of decision making. Everyone will know of someone who is a Christian at that point. Currently at 3 percent, we are still considered by most Manhattan residents an oddity not to be taken seriously."[20]

Reaching this goal will change not only New York City; it will change America. The three arenas of cultural influence—morals, aesthetics and knowledge—will be affected as more Christians enter them. There is a great possibility that this can happen as God brings Christians from the Global South to New York City—50 percent of the Asian immigrants are Christian, thousands of Hispanic churches have been established, and African churches are being established by the dozens.[21]

To reach that goal, denominations, congregations and networks that are serious about this mission will prayerfully consider a ten-year church-planting goal. Infrastructure is in place to provide coaching and networking for new church planters. An alliance of like-minded denominations has been collaborating for a decade by praying together and sharing resources to catalyze a movement of church planting.

LEADER APPLICATION

- Reflect on God's grace in your life and identify three to five things God has given you that you do not deserve or did not expect to receive (e.g., spiritual life, calling, abilities, resources, sacred relationships). How have they changed your life?

- Identify communities in your city that need to experience the grace of God (e.g., single-parent families, the unemployed, the homeless, prison inmates, anyone far from God). Pray for these groups and be open to hear God tell you what you might do to take his message of grace to them.

- If a friend or an acquaintance is planting a church, consider ways you could be an encouragement.

A prayer . . .

Jesus,

Thank you for grace. Create in me a deeper awareness of how your grace is at work in my life. May the abundance of your grace spill over to places in my community where it has not yet been seen.

TIM KELLER'S MAJOR LIFE EVENTS

1972	Graduates from Bucknell College
1975	Graduates from Gordon-Conwell Theological Seminary
1989	Plants Redeemer Presbyterian Church
1993	Redeemer grows to 1,500 attendees
2000	Redeemer grows to 2,000 attendees
2005	Redeemer grows to 3,600 attendees
2008	Publishes *Reason for God* and *Prodigal God*
2009	Publishes *Counterfeit God*; Redeemer City to City is established
2010	Speaks at Lausanne Congress
2011	Publishes *King's Cross*; Redeemer grows to 5,400 attendees

Luis Palau

FESTIVAL!

*Preaching Boldly—Through Word and Deed—
to Billions of People*

LEARN: Bold faith changes not only individuals and churches but also nations and continents.

SUCCEED: Be an evangelist who proclaims the gospel fearlessly and creatively.

Open hostility to the gospel does not deter Luis Palau. He sees every obstacle as an opportunity for God to do what Luis and his colleagues cannot. In the spring of 2011, due to the efforts of a passionate Vietnamese Christian, Palau preached the gospel to thousands of people in Ho Chi Minh City, the largest city in communist Vietnam. "It was the first time in Vietnam's history that an international Christian leader was able to preach the Gospel to such a large audience since 1975, when the country became communist."[1]

Palau was one of the first bicultural, immigrant evangelists to understand American evangelicalism. Born in Argentina, he nonetheless knows how to communicate the gospel in the U.S. despite the challenges and complexities of the American church.

By the time I heard Palau preach in 1996 at the Promise Keepers rally in Shea Stadium, he had been considered the "Billy Graham of Latin America" for more than twenty years. I also heard him speak at the Urbana Student Missions Conference hosted by Inter-Varsity Christian Fellowship in 1981.

In 2001, I met Kevin Palau, Luis's son and now president of the Luis Palau Association (LPA). We were exploring the possibility of fulfilling a lifetime dream of his father—to conduct an evangelistic outreach in New York City. During our conversation, Kevin told me about his father's desire to see American cities host festivals, a new form of outreach adopted by the LPA. Kevin was traveling on behalf of the LPA to explore on behalf of his father and the agency some future potential opportunities in the New York City area.

In November 2010, I traveled to Portland, Oregon, to visit with Kevin at the LPA offices. John Volinsky, a World Vision colleague, was traveling with me to work on a possible collaboration between World Vision and the Palau organization.

During an appreciation luncheon for volunteers and supporters, we watched a video of Luis Palau's 2010 meeting in Chile. He was with Jose Henriquez, the Chilean miner who had been trapped underground with coworkers for sixty-nine days. Henriquez had been the "community pastor" for the thirty-three trapped miners. He led prayer meetings and had them listen to tapes of Palau. Henriquez led many of the miners to make personal faith commitments during the dark days when death seemed imminent. By watching the video it was obvious that Luis Palau has maintained a unique gifting to preach the gospel in diverse contexts even after forty years of circling the globe.

Kevin Palau has led an effort with the New York City Leadership Center, Redeemer City to City and Mission Houston to create a learning community among leaders from maturing city movements. Leaders from Atlanta, Boston, Chicago, Dallas, Denver, Houston, New York City, Phoenix, Portland and San Diego have committed to meet together every year for five years in New York City. The Palau organization also created a website (www. gospelmovements.org) to highlight what God is doing in cities as the result of united spiritual movements.

In addition to Kevin, Luis has two other sons who are part of the association. Keith, Kevin's twin, works in donor development. And Andrew, after a season of drifting away from God, has followed his father's footsteps and become an evangelist.

DEFINING MOMENTS

Palau's parents did not grow up in Christian families. They came to Christ as a result of the witness of Edward Rogers, a vice president of Shell Oil Company. Soon after turning their lives over to the Lord, they became involved with the Plymouth Brethren Church, and Palau's father became a passionate lay evangelist, preaching on the street and handing out Bibles.

When Luis Palau was only ten years old, his father died, leaving his mother with six children to raise—Palau and five younger sisters.

Palau remembers his father's final moments. He was having difficulty breathing, but suddenly he "sat up and began to sing, while clapping: 'Bright crowns up there, bright crowns for you and me. Then the palm of victory, the palm of victory.' After singing this song three times, he fell back onto his bed and announced, 'I'm going to be with Jesus, which is far better.'"[2]

His father's death molded Palau's worldview. "Seeing him die at such a young age has given me a lifelong sense of urgency," Palau has said.[3] "My father was my hero as a boy. His pride in the Gospel and boldness to share it with others deeply marked my life. His death molded my whole view of life, eternity, death, and the future."[4]

Palau was twelve when he was invited by Charles Cohen, his

teacher and cricket coach, to attend a Christian youth camp. Cohen was a Jewish Christian who knew that Palau had not yet made a commitment to Christ. Palau thought he could get out of going by saying that his family couldn't afford it, but Cohen offered to pay. Palau's camp counselor was Frank Chandler, who spoke individually with each of his campers about their spiritual condition.

Palau was unsuccessful at avoiding his turn to talk with the counselor, and Chandler asked him probing questions about his relationship with Christ. Then Chandler read Romans 10:9-10: "If you confess with your mouth, 'Jesus is Lord,' and believe in your heart that God raised him from the dead, you will be saved. For it is with your heart that you believe and are justified, and it is with your mouth that you confess and are saved" (NIV 1984). After asking a few more questions, Chandler led Palau to a point of confessing Christ as Lord.[5] For Palau, the link between faith and bold proclamation of that faith was forged at the moment of his conversion. After that, no one would ever use the word *timid* to describe Palau. He has spent the rest of his life boldly confessing that Jesus is Lord.

By age seventeen, Palau was recognized as an evangelist. He spoke at boys' clubs and led meetings for children and young adults. At age twenty he purchased a tent and preached all summer in Cordoba, Argentina. He spent every Wednesday night with Keith Bentson, a missionary with Servicio Evangelizador Para America Latina, in extended sessions of prayer for the world. "Those prayer meetings in Keith's office revolutionized my life," Palau said. "My vision for those who needed Christ became international, geographical and global."[6]

Palau's faith was formed by Scripture memorization, a spiritual discipline he learned from Edward Rogers. Early on he memorized Matthew 6:33: "Seek first his kingdom and his righteousness, and all these things will be given to you as well." Palau was determined to seek first God's kingdom and to leave "all these things," whatever they might be, in God's hands.

His belief in that verse was put to the test when his mother challenged him to quit his job and pursue a career as an evangelist. "I was working at a British bank in Argentina, and my mother used to say, 'Leave the bank. Preach the gospel. Plant churches.' I replied, 'Mom, I'm waiting for the call.' She exclaimed, 'The call went out two thousand years ago! The Lord's not waiting for the call; He's waiting for the answer!'"[7]

Palau yielded to his mother's challenge and dedicated his life to become a missionary. He met Ray Stedman, a pastor from Palo Alto, California, while Ray was on a mission trip to Argentina. Stedman became Palau's spiritual father in America. Through Stedman's influence, a door opened for Palau to study at Multnomah School of the Bible in Portland, Oregon.

Studying in America proved to be challenging, and Palau became discouraged. He wanted to give up and go home. Did he really need a degree to preach the gospel? He could learn the Bible without a formal education. The Holy Spirit could teach him everything he needed to know. As he sat in chapel trying to justify the decision to quit school, God reminded him that he did not

BETWEEN 1965 AND 1980 PALAU PREACHED SIXTY-THREE CRUSADES IN SIXTEEN LATIN COUNTRIES:

Argentina	Honduras
Bolivia	Mexico
Colombia	Nicaragua
Costa Rica	Peru
Dominican Republic	Puerto Rico
Ecuador	Spain
El Salvador	Uruguay
Guatemala	Venezuela[9]

need to do anything in his own strength. Palau realized, "It is not I but Christ in me."[8] Finishing his education was an important step in learning to let Christ do what Palau could not.

Before graduating, Palau met and married classmate Patricia Marilyn Scofield. They finished school and joined Overseas Crusade in 1962.

Palau worked for Overseas Crusade for twenty years. He served as the team director in Costa Rica, Colombia and Mexico. He also served as president of Overseas Crusade from 1974 to 1976, giving oversight to 150 missionaries.

In the 1970s, Billy Graham and Palau began to establish a relationship. Having learned of Palau's impact throughout Latin America, Graham invited him to speak at the 1974 Lausanne Congress in Switzerland. By giving him that opportunity, Palau says, Graham "established a lot of trust between me and leaders from around the world."[10]

The Palau-Graham relationship went through three phases: hero, mentor, and partner.[11] As Palau was beginning his work as an evangelist, Billy Graham was his hero. Not only was Graham recognized worldwide as an evangelist, but he was also respected. Graham became Palau's mentor when he invited Palau to participate in one of his crusades. In 1974, Palau shared his testimony at a Graham crusade in Phoenix. When Palau started his own organization, the Luis Palau Evangelistic Association (LPEA), Graham became his partner by providing a seed contribution of $100,000.

After establishing the LPEA, Palau began to preach outside of Latin America. In 1977, he preached for six weeks in Wales. In 1986, he preached in Singapore, and his messages were translated into seventeen languages for sixty thousand people nightly in a national football stadium.[12]

During a breakfast conversation in 1983, Graham challenged Palau to focus on cities where the greatest numbers of people live.

That year Palau and Graham both conducted campaigns in England. Palau preached to more than 500,000 people over the course of fifty days in ten locations in Greater London, while Graham preached to more than one million people throughout the country. As a result of their combined efforts, more than 125,000 people made recorded commitments to Christ.[13]

Prior to 1990 Palau was reluctant to preach in the United States because he did not want to compete with Graham. But in 1990, Graham encouraged Palau to come. After that, Palau invested 50 percent of his time in the United States.

Palau found the state of Christianity in the U.S. deeply troubling. "The disunity of the churches in America has created enormous obstacles to overcome," he said. "It is very difficult for the gospel to go forth when leaders cannot work together. The perception of evangelicalism is that it is harsh, judgmental and uninviting."[14]

Given the spiritual climate in America and the adverse attitude toward large-scale evangelistic crusades, the Palau organization birthed a new model they call festivals. The idea was to use acts of service to express the gospel in cities.

The first festival, held in Portland in 1999, attracted more than ninety thousand people over two days. Churches were mobilized to serve the city in a range of community-based projects. At a culminating rally in Portland, recognized as one of the least-churched cities in the U.S., more than 100,000 people came out to hear Palau preach.[15]

CONSEQUENTIAL IMPACT

Latin America. Dr. Roy Fish from Southwestern Baptist Theological Seminary said that Luis Palau, next to Mr. Graham, "stands taller in the ministry of crusade evangelism than any of his contemporaries." Fish acknowledges that Palau does not appear to be anything extraordinary, "yet God uses him as an instrument through which He changes cities all across the world."[16]

Palau's career parallels the enormous spiritual changes in Latin

America. In 2001, *Time* magazine reported: "Astonishingly, there are almost certainly more Brazilian Protestants in church on Sundays than Catholics. Protestants boast a minimum of twenty million churchgoers and are expanding twice as fast as the overall population."[17] This is a remarkable statement given that Brazil and Mexico have the largest percentage of Catholics of any country in the world.

The Protestants in Brazil have increased from an estimated 9 percent of the population in 1991 to as high as 22 percent in 2006. Protestant growth in Latin America is connected to the growth of cities, where Protestant churches are reaching out to new arrivals who are disoriented and lonely. As a result, many immigrants are finding a spiritual home in evangelical churches.[18]

A 2004 estimate indicated that 15 percent of Latin America has been converted to evangelical Christianity, making it the fastest-growing religion in the region. The Latin America Catholic Bishops Conference claimed that eight thousand Latin Americans convert to evangelical Christianity every day. In Guatemala, the evangelical population is now more than 20 percent. The preaching of Palau and others has found a receptive audience in cities and among the poor. According to one report from Venezuela, "The change in new converts is breathtaking."[19]

The Palau organization has changed the perception of evangelical Christianity in Latin America. In October 2010, 145,000 people attended the Palau Festival in Chile. On the Saturday of the event, Palau wore the shirt that Jose Henriquez was wearing when he was pulled from the mine after being trapped for sixty-nine days. Henriquez was so moved by the presence of Palau in Chile that he gave his shirt to Palau as a gesture of gratitude. Palau used the shirt to convey the message about spiritual rescue. During the trip, Palau and his son Andrew met with President Sebastian Pinera, who was at the site when the miners were pulled out.[20]

Palau is not shy about speaking the truth of God's Word to anyone. His message is the same to the rich and the poor, the weak and the powerful. In every major meeting in Latin America the media and public officials want to participate. Well-known converts include two presidents of Bolivia: Hugo Banzer and Juan Pereda Ashun.[21]

Global impact. In 1950, as a young man of sixteen, Palau was taking care of a widowed mother and five sisters. In the next fifty years he preached the gospel in over seventy countries. He preached in the United States for the first time in 1970, in Spain for the first time in 1973 and in India for the first time in 1988.[22] Palau had long dreamed of preaching in China. The dream was realized in 2000 when he preached in Shanghai. Palau returned to China in 2004.

In 2008, Palau preached to his largest audience—850,000 in Buenos Aires. His longest events were in Chicago (fifty-seven days in 1996) and London (fifty days in 1983).

Palau described the results of the London meetings: "People of every creed, color, religious background, and walk of life trusted Jesus Christ—a member of the royal family, a top rock star, a famous actress, a disillusioned policeman, a car dealer, a truck driver, and a bus driver interviewed that same night by BBC."[23]

The impact of Palau's bold proclamation of the gospel is realized not only in the number of people turning to Christ, but in the unity of believers and churches. According to Palau, many leaders identify unity among Christians as one of the most exciting results of the campaigns.

Not only are existing churches strengthened, but new churches are planted. More than four thousand churches in different corners of the world had been planted by 2007. In Romania alone, one thousand new churches were started after the 1990 and 1991 campaigns with eighty-five thousand public declarations of faith. In Uganda one hundred new churches were started between 2005 and 2007, largely through the preaching of Andrew Palau and the cooperating churches.

The impact on participating churches is equally remarkable. According to the Palau organization, churches actively involved in one of their crusades "receive seven times more growth afterward than a church that holds back and doesn't train its people to be friendship evangelists, counselors, and follow-up workers."[24]

The festival model. Under the leadership of Kevin Palau, five hundred churches in Portland have been involved in a Season of Service, the model launched in 1999. The efforts of the churches include feeding the homeless, providing free medical care, fixing up local schools and offering supplies to low-income students— all done with no strings attached.

The new paradigm has received attention from major news sources, including *USA Today*. Reporter Tom Krattenmaker writes, "What is new and different about the Season of Service [is the] emphasis on 'preaching' through idealistic action rather than pious words."[25] A *Christianity Today* article in 2001 acknowledged the effectiveness of the new model.[26]

A SPIRITUAL AWAKENING IN NORTH AMERICAN CITIES

Building on the vision of his father, Kevin Palau is working with colleagues from other cities—Tom White in Corvallis, Oregon, Glenn Barth in Minneapolis, Jim Herrington in Dallas, Scott Chapman in Chicago, Glenn Smith in Montréal, Sam Williams in San Diego, and Mac Pier in New York—to steward a vision of city leaders working together to bring spiritual awakening to their communities.

In an annual Movement Day gathering, leaders of large U.S. cities come together to encourage one another, coach one another and see what God is doing in other cities. As churches plant other churches and minister to their cities, they report good results in difficult areas, including public education and sex trafficking.

The foundation of this movement was laid by historic prayer movements in nearly every city.

Kevin Palau has taken up his father's sense of urgency. Described as the "new face" of evangelicalism by Krattenmaker, Palau believes in serving before speaking, and he is earning a hearing for the gospel of Christ in places that have a distorted view of the Christian faith.

VISION

Nearly thirty years ago, Billy Graham challenged Luis Palau to go to the cities. Palau and his sons are being faithful to that charge. Kevin has a vision to use the good will created from fifty years of his father's global travel to preach the gospel where the need and the potential are the greatest—in large cities that have global influence. The Palaus speak of planting the festival model in one hundred cities worldwide.

They speak with equal passion about the need to unite the church. Luis Palau is troubled by the inability of churches to work together on any significant scale. He is hopeful that churches can be united at unprecedented levels to serve their communities. They are seeing this begin to happen as a result of the three-part festival model: season of service; two-day festival; long-term involvement. Instead of a one-time preaching event, the Palaus are using long-term relationships to win people and communities to Christ.

Palau and his sons have a great vision for emerging evangelists. Because Luis was the beneficiary of many mentoring relationships, the Luis Palau Association now identifies and mobilizes thousands of new evangelists. The organization also provides regular opportunities for young evangelists to be mentored by those in leadership—in particular, Andrew Palau.

The Palau organization wants to expand its efforts in Asia, where more than one half of the world population lives. It is particularly keen on doing more work in China and India. Within twenty years, near the one hundredth birthday of Luis Palau, they envision all of the major cities on the globe having festivals as an annual expression of what Jesus would do—serve the needy and speak words of truth and healing to the multitudes.[27]

LEADER APPLICATION

- Identify two areas where you need to exercise courage and boldness for the sake of the gospel (e.g., home, work, school, community, a difficult place in your city). What might that courage and boldness look like?

- What service could you offer as a way of creatively sharing your faith?

A prayer . . .

Jesus,

Show me ways I can demonstrate your love through service to my community. I ask for boldness and courage and for vision to find others who will join me.

LUIS PALAU'S MAJOR EVENTS

1965-1969	Latin America	16 campaigns in 6 countries
1970	United States	First meeting
1973	Europe	First meeting—Spain
1986	Asia	First meeting—Singapore
1990	India	First meeting
1996 1983	Longest meetings	Chicago—57 days London—50 days
2000	China	First meeting
2008 1998	Largest meetings	Buenos Aires—850,000 Egypt—555,000

4

A. R. Bernard

CULTURE

A Vision to See Christianity Transform Society

LEARN: Understand how Christianity transcends and influences culture.

SUCCEED: Encourage people to live out their God-given calling in the context of culture.

For more than fifteen years I have had the privilege of partnering with A. R. Bernard on diverse initiatives. Together with a community of New York City faith leaders, we cohosted the one-month 9/11 memorial in October 2001, the final Billy Graham Crusade in 2005 and the launch of the New York City Leadership Center at the Christian Cultural Center.

I first crossed paths with Bernard in 1995 at Bethel Gospel Assembly in Harlem. He arrived to participate in a luncheon with Ray Bakke, a world-renowned Christian urbanologist.[1] We were planning a New York City urban consultation called "Gatekeepers '95."

By that time, Bernard was regularly speaking to audiences of fifty thousand men in football stadiums across the nation as part of the Promise Keepers movement. His messages were challenging yet empowering: he challenged men to live lives of integrity and then helped them believe that with Christ's power they could do it.

Bernard also convinced his audiences of the importance of becoming leaders in movements of racial reconciliation. His messages were making him one of the most well-known African American Christian leaders in the nation. Promise Keepers hosted 35,000 men at Shea Stadium in Flushing, Queens, in 1995. It was the most racially diverse event of the Promise Keepers movement.

In the fall of that year, Bernard and I, in conjunction with Concerts of Prayer Greater New York, cohosted a ministry leaders' conference at his church. With a focus on racial reconciliation, the conference was a follow-up gathering for pastors from the Shea Stadium event. It was the first time that our two organizations worked together to cohost an event.

One week before Bernard spoke at the Movement Day Conference in New York City in September 2011, he and I met at the Tick Tock Diner on 34th and 8th Avenue. When I asked him to tell me his biggest passion, he said, "I see myself as an institution builder. I want to inspire other leaders to see themselves not just as pastors or missionaries but to understand the role of our institutions in our society."

Bernard's love for learning makes him one of the most inquisitive leaders I know. His intellectual and crosscultural agility is impressive, and his ability to build a powerful faith institution in New York City is unprecedented.

DEFINING MOMENTS

Bernard was born in Panama to a single mother. When he was four years of age, his family moved to Brooklyn. Since youth, he has been a hard worker. At the age of sixteen he was pushing clothes racks in Manhattan's garment district for two dollars per hour. He took a brief, moral detour to explore the dark world of drug dealing, but set it aside in pursuit of God, truth and reality. This pursuit led him to a five-year relationship with the Nation of Islam, a Black Muslim movement. At the same time, a college-bound program in his high school introduced him to "a promising career in finance. He eventually landed a respected position at Banker's Trust Company."[2]

While Bernard was working as the unit head for the Consumer Lending Division, a bank secretary witnessed to him. Her persistent and childlike faith in Jesus Christ disarmed him. In the Nation of Islam, he found discipline and identity but nothing like the personal relationship with God that this woman spoke about.

She invited him to attend a meeting at the Baptist Temple in January 1975, and he accepted. Nicky Cruz, a well-known convert to Christianity whose story was told by David Wilkerson in *The Cross and the Switchblade,* was the speaker. That evening, Bernard heard God speak to his spirit as with the "power of a blow torch through his chest." Bernard heard God say to him, "I am the God you are looking for. I and My Word are one."[3]

Up to that point Bernard had viewed Christianity as a tool of oppression and a refuge for the weak. His only involvement with any church was to attend social activities or participate in sports. But that all changed when God powerfully revealed himself in the person of Christ. Bernard dove into Scripture and soon came to understand the vast difference between the institution of Christianity and the person of Christ. One year later Bernard accepted God's call to ministry, and in 1978 he and his wife, Karen,[4] launched a storefront church.[5]

The church that the couple founded has become one of the greatest spiritual and architectural achievements in New York City in the past century. The congregation has grown to 35,000 registered members and 15,000 weekly attendees. It is easily the largest congregation between Washington, D. C., and Maine, and one of the largest churches in the nation.

Another defining moment for Bernard took place nine years later when a New York City official informed Bernard that the Office of Clergy Liaison was being disbanded while the liaison for the Jewish and Muslim communities was not. Bernard recalled in an interview that when he asked why, the official responded, "Judaism and Islam represent a culture, whereas Christianity is just a religion." That statement rocked Bernard's world and became the catalyst that formed his understanding of Christianity as a culture.

After years of study and deliberate conversations with his congregation, Bernard developed a new paradigm for how the church can engage culture and society. His understanding of Christ's transcendent relationship to society was the driving force behind the next two decades of extraordinary growth.

People flocked to hear his life-transforming messages. In a decade, the church grew to eleven thousand. On a typical Sunday morning in the 1990s, people would stand in lines around the block to get into one of four Sunday morning services. The church grew by 1,000 members or more per year to reach its current membership of 35,000.[6]

CONSEQUENTIAL IMPACT

The impact of Bernard's leadership is rooted in this main idea: Every Christian is called to engage culture from a biblical worldview.

Bernard preaches the absolute centrality of a God-centered faith that transcends culture rather than opposes it. Having come out of a fundamentalist background that saw the church as standing against culture, Bernard came to believe instead that people are called to engage culture as a spiritual responsibility and as part of their spiritual formation.

BERNARD TALKS ABOUT FIVE COMPETING WORLDVIEWS AT WORK IN CULTURE.

Naturalism. This atheistic, secularist view of the world is prevalent in greater New York where the affluent are unreceptive to spirituality.

Pantheism. The belief that God is in everything is increasing in New York, especially among people from parts of Asia.

Postmodernism. The idea that objective truth cannot be known is popular among the 500,000 university students in greater New York.

Spiritism/polytheism. The belief that people can have many "gods" is practiced subconsciously by modern New Yorkers who have competing allegiances to deities ranging from spiritual gods to material gods.

Theism. The belief in the One God of Abraham is represented by large populations of Christians, Jews and Muslims.

Bernard has devoted his life to practicing this call, as evidenced by numerous awards and accomplishments. His influence is visible in three primary settings: church, community and world.

Church: The Christian Cultural Center. While on a walking tour of the Christian Cultural Center, Bernard said to me, "CCC is a Christ-centered church that spans diverse pillars of influence—government, business, education—and a broad socioeconomic spectrum of leaders from professional athletes to local residents. The church," he explained, "is a blend of ancient spiritual themes and modern technology. We use everything from paintings, original art and historical artifacts to banners and an aquarium." By thoughtfully and purposefully using all of these, Bernard and his church combine the power of beauty and truth in creative expressions of worship. Each aspect expresses the purpose of the Center: to convey the transforming power of Christ in culture.

Bernard leads his congregation of 35,000 with the help of 100 full-time staff and 1,500 volunteers. The core message of the Christian Cultural Center is that every believer has a vocation. The church is organized around a combination of small groups and vocational affinity groups. Staff members make every effort to link Christians by vocation and geography.

Bernard spends a half day every two months with his entire staff to invest in their development. He also provides regular training opportunities for all of his volunteers to teach them the values and mission of the church. He has taken his entire volunteer force to Disney World in Orlando to study the principles of excellence in customer service. Bernard is a consummate developer of people and organizations.

Bernard lists five purposes of the Christian Cultural Center: worship, community, maturity, leadership and mission. On the surface, these look generic. They could apply to most American congregations. Yet the challenge of putting these into practice in inner-city Brooklyn is anything but generic. The five purposes are woven into the visual design of the church building—through murals, flat-screen television presentations and a room with the purposes stated in detail. They take on programmatic expression within the church through Sunday morning services, uniquely crafted discipleship modules and the expectation that the staff team is constantly being stretched to innovate their programs.

New York City is the most spiritually diverse city in the world. Every major form of religious belief and unbelief exists in astonishing numbers. Greater New York City includes nine of the twenty-five most populous Muslim counties in America.[7]

The religious and cultural diversity of New York City, coupled with enormous spiritual and socioeconomic challenges, creates a challenging context for leadership. One of Bernard's gifts is his ability to navigate so many belief systems. In New York City, conversations about faith and race are an important part of the relational landscape. More than 90 percent of active Christians are Hispanic, African American, Caribbean American or Asian.

In a May 2009 *New York Times* interview, Bernard recounted several episodes that confirm his conviction that God acts in supernatural ways among our most challenged citizens. "Listen, I don't teach that God is some genie in a lamp and you rub the Bible three times and he pops out," he said. "But the Bible gives hope. That's what we deal in. That hope sometimes transfers into miracles."[8]

Bernard and his team have birthed a number of holistic initiatives, including a food pantry, prison ministry, domestic violence initiative and a male mentoring program. Bernard's commitment to male mentoring is one of his greatest contributions to Christianity in modeling how to effectively engage men. In urban churches, male attendance is often as low as 20 percent. Bernard has consistently attracted male involvement of 50 percent. The mentoring initiative involves more than one thousand male mentors.

Each person who attends the Christian Cultural Center is expected to progress through four stages of discipleship: (1) Seekers find God's grace; (2) followers understand and apply God's Word; (3) learners experience self-discovery regarding gifts and calling; (4) ambassadors articulate and share their faith.[9]

Bernard's vision for the Christian Cultural Center is ambitious. He sees it as a fusion of cathedral, Smithsonian Institute and college campus—in other words, the integration of the sacred, the institutional and the intellectual.

Sacred. The worship space accommodates nearly four thousand congregants in a "vibrant, modern and aesthetically energizing" environment.[10] The cathedral theme has been effective—former Catholics make up 37 percent of recent growth.

Bernard is a big believer in the "third space" concept—a place where "people find community apart from home and work. In this 'third space' people [encounter God and] are welcomed into a life of spiritual growth and personal mission."[11]

Institutional. Partnering with seminaries and cultural institutions, the Christian Cultural Center displays original and ancient biblical literature, manuscripts and artifacts. In the same area is a photograph from the Via Dolorosa in Jerusalem, a place Bernard toured with leaders from Alliance Theological Seminary.

Intellectual. Bernard's vision for the church as a classroom is seen in his work with young people. Synergies for Success is an after-school program in which parents, mentors and teachers partner to lift young people academically. As many as one hundred adults are involved in this partnership.

Bernard recognizes the importance of reaching junior high and high school students, so the young people have their own dedicated worship space. A café has also been created as a safe space for them. Bernard's son Jamaal oversees the program.

Bernard and his team have been involved in an intense, five-year research effort to create a large-scale spiritual coaching model. He has brought together the pastoral staff, theologians and professional psychologists to create a seven-track model. When the plan is operational, every full-time staff member will participate in a self-assessment and then be placed on the appropriate track. Each track has a specific curriculum—including Scripture, books, seminars, fellowship groups, conferences, articles and commentary—that will guide people through measurable steps toward spiritual growth and maturity. An accountability vehicle is built in to gauge participation.

Community: New York City. The Christian Cultural Center has become an important meeting destination for churches and their leaders. It is often used as a gathering place for citywide religious events.

One month after the tragedy of 9/11, Bernard hosted, before a grieving nation, a nationally televised memorial for the victims. One of the testimonies came from a pregnant, grieving widow whose husband was one of six hundred employees killed from the firm of Cantor Fitzgerald. She represented the "face" of 9/11: a real person, not a statistic, whose life was violently changed by the tragedy.

Bernard has also hosted broadcasts for the National Day of Prayer, the Willow Creek Leadership Summit and a screening for one of the Narnia movies.

In 2006 Bernard became president of the New York City Council of Churches. The council has a rich history dating back to its founding in 1895. It has been linked to such historic figures as Presidents Teddy Roosevelt and John F. Kennedy. Today the council represents 1.5 million Protestant, Orthodox and Anglican Christians in New York City.

When Bernard became involved, the council had been somewhat stagnant for several decades. He saw an opportunity to revive the historic purposes of the council.

THE NYC COUNCIL OF CHURCHES
Four Historic Purposes

Advocacy—to raise critical issues in the public square with, and on behalf of, its churches and members. Issues include homelessness, low-cost housing, poverty and welfare programs. Roundtable discussions are held with corporate and nonprofit leaders.

Recognition—to honor Christian leaders in New York City whose ministry and service display courageous pioneering demonstrated by lifetime achievements.

Pastoral care and chaplains—to certify pastoral counselors and chaplains.

Educational opportunities for Christian leaders—to host an annual conference with world-renowned leaders to provide continuing education and networking opportunities.[12]

On May 18, 2005, when Bernard was vice president, the New York City Council of Churches hosted Dr. David Yonggi Cho, pastor of the largest congregation in the world. He was awarded the Family of Man Medallion. He was the twenty-fifth recipient; others have included John F. Kennedy, Dwight D. Eisenhower, Richard Nixon and Jimmy Carter.

Through his leadership role on the council, Bernard influences the broad spectrum of New York City's faith community. Every quarter, leaders of Catholic and Protestant, Jewish, and Muslim communities meet together as members of the three "Abrahamic" faiths.[13] Bernard considers this an opportunity to work together on "common grace" issues that affect the whole city—issues like housing and education.

The council is a neutral place where Bernard can galvanize the rapidly growing independent, Pentecostal and immigrant churches springing up in New York City. On a trip to Asia, he was able to meet with the leader of the Chinese Council of Churches. In New York City he is able to meet with leaders from thirty-five Indonesian congregations.

Apart from the council, Bernard is involved with strategic issues and leaders across the city. He led an effort to address the needs of a local community in the Starrett City housing projects—one of the largest in the nation. He served on Mayor Bloomberg's transition team and was the first citywide leader to endorse Bloomberg's third mayoral run. Bernard also founded the Brooklyn Preparatory School and has served on the New York City Economic Development Board and on the New York City Chancellor Advisory Cabinet.[14] Most recently he joined the Advisory Board for the New York City Male Initiative.

World: An Asian apostolic assignment. In recent years, an opportunity emerged for Bernard to influence leaders throughout Asia with the message of Christ and culture. "One of my greatest delights in the past few years has been the opportunity to travel internationally and share what we have learned with leaders in Asia," Bernard said in an interview. "The message of Christ in culture has universal appeal." Recognizing the growing influence of Asia over the rest of the globe, as well as its rapidly growing Christian community, Bernard has been drawn to Singapore—an island nation, which, like Manhattan, is a gateway to much of the continent. Bernard describes Singapore as a nation wrestling with a rapidly changing religious landscape. The emergence of a strong Christian community, bringing social as well as religious change, has been a challenge for governmental leaders.

Bernard has traveled extensively to Singapore, Taiwan, New Zealand, Australia, Indonesia, Malaysia and Hong Kong. In each context he has taught thousands of ministry and marketplace leaders the principles of influencing culture. He has worked with many young Christian movements, providing invaluable perspective on institution building.

In response to his teaching and influence, a number of leaders have taken on pressing social issues such as AIDS and health care. Bernard has pressed these leaders to focus on integrity, character and giving back to the community. As a result, programs and clinics are beginning to emerge that meet the social needs of communities—all motivated by a Christ-centered faith committed to engaging the local community.

During his 2009 trip to several Asian nations, Bernard trained a total of 15,000 leaders. His largest audience was 3,500 leaders. Bernard's message is transformational in nations where governments are openly hostile to the Christian community. His message to leaders in the United States and Asia is simply this—God's grace is reflected in culture, and we need to understand the relationship between faith and culture. Culture can be transformed by people of faith who are conversant with culture.[15]

VISION

Bernard has a passion to educate. In 2010 he opened a charter school with an innovative model that creates an amazing educational culture among students and faculty. The school is housed on the CCC campus with grades K-3 and is expected to grow to K-12 within the next five years. Charter schools are crucial to urban centers. More than 60 percent of New York City's 1.1 million public school students are performing below standard math and reading levels.

Bernard also envisions the birth of a new, innovative form of urban seminary that will complement training already available in the city and be accessible to inner-city leaders. Given the limited seminary resources in greater New York, this vision is crucial. According to an estimate by Dr. Dale Irwin, president of New York Theological seminary, only fifteen thousand leaders in this region of 21.5 million people are matriculated in seminaries.

Bernard said in an interview that he senses an urgent need for leaders to provide what he calls an "incarnational expression of dynamic orthodoxy." To people living in the shadow of enormous urban challenges, Christ must become increasingly real. Bernard believes that leaders formed in this new kind of seminary will be equipped to lead dynamic churches and organizations with passion and skill.

Bernard's passion is to see hundreds of thousands of Christians fully engage their vocational call to government, education, economics, mass media, arts and entertainment. Urban America is vocationally focused. The majority of New York City residents are there because of their vocations. They spend the majority of their waking hours either working or commuting to work. Bernard believes the city will flourish when Christians exercise their spiritual call and gifts in the context of their vocational callings. Bernard is convinced that well-led churches with clear teaching on engaging Christ and culture can effect a revolution.[16]

The story of A. R. Bernard is a picture of how God can transform one person's life. As the son of an immigrant single mother,

Bernard did not start out with the advantages that many consider essential for leadership. But God patiently pursued him. Then God passionately transformed him by enlarging his heart, his mind and his scope of influence over our nation's largest city. Bernard has a similar passion to see others transformed by the message that God entrusted to him. Through good stewardship, he is working to pass along to the next generation everything that he has learned and achieved in the past three decades. In a sense, Bernard's life symbolizes what he expects to see happen in and through the churches in New York City.

LEADER APPLICATION

- Identify at least one way that Christianity has influenced your city (e.g., schools, hospitals, political life, community engagement through local churches). How would your community be different with no Christian influence?

- Craft a one-sentence mission statement that defines your God-given calling to your vocation (e.g., God has called me to serve the immigrants of my community as a health care worker).

A prayer . . .

Jesus,

I pray for an awakening to my calling. Help me to integrate my faith and my vocation to influence my culture.

A. R. BERNARD'S MAJOR LIFE EVENTS

1953	Born in Panama
1957	Immigrates to Brooklyn, New York
1969	Clerk at Banker's Trust
1975	Conversion to Christ
1976	Call to ministry

1978	Plants storefront church in Brooklyn
1985	Church grows to 325—relocates to Greenpoint, Brooklyn
1989	Church relocates to Linden Boulevard in Canarsie, Brooklyn, with 625 members
1993	Founds Brooklyn Preparatory School
1997	Speaks to one million men on the Mall in Washington, D.C., during the national Promise Keepers rally
1999	Church has grown to 11,000 members
2005	Chairs the last Billy Graham Crusade in Flushing, Queens
2006	Named president of the New York City Council of Churches, which represents 1.5 million Protestants, Anglicans and Orthodox Christians in New York City
2007	Church grows to 29,000; Bernard receives a Lifetime Achievement Award by Consulate General of Israel in New York in conjunction with the Jewish Community Relations Council and Jewish National Fund
2008	Named most influential NYC Clergy and second most influential African American; Crain's New York Business magazine names Bernard as one of the "25 Leaders Reshaping New York"
2009	Teaches 15,000 leaders in Asia in multicountry trip

5

Glenn Smith

SHALOM

Seeking the Reconciliation of the Church to Transform the City

LEARN: God desires to bring shalom (peace) to our cities through well-trained and networked urban leaders.

SUCCEED: Strong personal foundations—healthy families, enduring friendships, deep spirituality—are essential for peaceful communities.

For more than thirty years, Glenn Smith has been observing the relationship between poverty and shalom. He has concluded that poverty is about more than economic scarcity; it's about relationships. People become impoverished when they have inadequate access to social, emotional, physical and financial resources. The lives of people without relationships unravel in all of these areas.[1]

Smith and I were introduced to one another by Ray Bakke, a mutual friend and mentor. Ray recruited both of us, ten years apart, to study with him in doctoral programs. Smith studied at Northern Baptist Theological Seminary in Chicago; I studied in Philadelphia at Eastern Baptist Theological Seminary.

When we met for the first time and started to get acquainted, I was amazed by the overlapping influences in our lives—common mentors, common passion for the city and common yearning for the church in those cities to flourish. Smith's relationship to Montréal paralleled my relationship to New York. As the executive director of Christian Direction (a faith-based nonprofit in Montréal committed to the shalom of the city), he recognized the intimate relationship between Montréal, Boston and New York City—cities with a strong Catholic influence and a declining spiritual life. I recognized Smith as a thoughtful leader with the gift of encouragement.

At the time of our meeting, Smith was also serving as the senior urban associate for the Lausanne Movement.[2] He was in charge of overseeing the afternoon seminars at Cape Town 2010, the Lausanne event in South Africa. Over an eighteen-month period, he and I attended meetings in New York City and Cape Town, South Africa, where I was privileged to attend Lausanne as a U.S. delegate.

As we sat in his office at the Cape Town Convention Center, Smith cast a vision for a gathering of leaders from the world's most influential cities. Recognizing the rapid growth of global cities, he said, "We need to bring leaders together who are wrestling with the specific challenges of urban ministry. We have much to learn from one another. Networking urban ministry practitioners is crucial to the maturation of spiritual movements in our cities."[3]

DEFINING MOMENTS

Smith grew up in downtown Toronto in a strongly Christian family. "My family had a huge passion for missions," Smith said, "especially for Asia." At the University of Michigan, Smith studied French literature, linguistics and religious studies. He later earned a master's degree in early Christian literature from the

University of Ottawa. He is fluent in both French and English.

After working as a university chaplain for nine years, in 1983 Smith became executive director of Christian Direction, an organization in Montréal that partners with churches to incarnate the love of God in neighborhoods throughout cities. His wife, Sandy, is involved in the organization as a church-community organizer.

Reading *Rich Christians in an Age of Hunger* by Ron Sider was a defining moment for Smith. Sider's book made him aware of the extremes of wealth and poverty in the Western Hemisphere.[4] He witnessed the devastating effects of poverty in 1979 when he went to Haiti on his first missions trip. The majority of people on the island nation live on less than two dollars a day. What started there became a thirty-year journey of training Haitian lay leaders.

Another defining moment for Smith was meeting Ray Bakke in 1987. Bakke invited Smith to study for a doctorate at Northern Baptist Theological Seminary in Chicago. For the next four years, Smith not only studied under Bakke but also grew a friendship with him. The relationship led to Smith's entering the world of global urban ministry.[5]

In his study of Scripture, Smith found four hundred biblical references that describe the Almighty as a God of justice. In Jewish writings and tradition, Smith says, *shalom* is "where justice and peace embrace." The concept of shalom occurs 236 times in the Old Testament and refers to a state of fulfillment resulting from God's presence and covenant relationship with his people.[6]

Smith has come to realize that urban needs are rooted in many types of poverty—relational, social and physical as well as financial. The antidote to poverty is close relationships that result in loving responses to people's needs. His relationship with Bakke and other mentors has forged Smith's philosophy and informed his practice of sustainable community development in urban areas.

Canada is one of the most urbanized countries on the planet. As Smith says, "The urban system of Canada *is* Canada."[7] Toronto,

Montréal and Vancouver occupy less than 1 percent of Canada's land mass but are home to 35 percent of the population. These cities are not only large, they are strategic. Vancouver is a major portal to Asia with its high concentration of Chinese residents. Montréal is a portal to the French-speaking world in Europe, the Caribbean and Africa. Migration between these global communities brings the world to Canada's doorstep.

Smith's daily commute takes him through the multilingual neighborhood of Chomedy, which is becoming increasingly Islamic. He walks past a Protestant church and through the parking lot of a Roman Catholic parish. "Forty years ago, both churches were full for weekend services," Smith says. "The United Church had a Sunday school that taught over two hundred children. The exodus of Anglophones from Montréal has decimated the congregation. Today, forty gather on Sunday at eleven a.m. for worship. The Roman Catholic parish once celebrated forty-five masses each week. Late last year, they sold the parish to an immigrant Armenian congregation."[8]

Montréal is the second most influential French-speaking city in the world after Paris. On a twelve-minute bus ride into downtown, Smith passes four major universities and thirty community colleges. Montréal has the most students per capita of any city in North America. Two hundred thousand elementary and secondary school students represent 168 countries.

"In 1700 fewer than 2 percent of the world's population lived in urban places. . . . By 1900 an estimated 9 percent of the world's population was urban. . . . In 1950, 27 percent of the world's population lived in cities. . . .

"By 1996 . . . better than 50 percent of the world's population lived in cities. By 2020 the urban population of Asia will be around 2.5 billion, having doubled in 25 years. By then more than half of the urban areas of the planet will be in Asia."[9]

Cities provide people in the developing world the best hope of education and income. They are the pump that keeps people circulating around the globe. Smith was startled to realize, however, that the rapid growth of cities is a matter of great spiritual concern. He describes Montréal as a "hurting city" with 238,000 people on the welfare rolls and 9,000 adolescent prostitutes. More than thirty-five tons of food are distributed daily to 150,000 people.[10]

CONSEQUENTIAL IMPACT

With his team in Montréal, Smith has created Twelve Key Indicators of a Transformed City. The framework is developed from four concentric circles. (See figure 5.1.)

Circle one: Reconciliation. Smith recognizes the local church as God's presence in a community. As such, churches are the hope of communities and the hope of the world. The degree to which churches are reconciled and collaborative determines their potential for good. Churches in the first circle perform acts of reconciliation with one another and the community.

Circle two: Evangelism and service. People use their gifts to demonstrate the good news of God, to create economic equality and to aid in language acquisition.

Circle three: Justice and forgiveness. By creating opportunities for the most vulnerable to reconnect with the city via educational opportunities, the city becomes a place where violence and sexual abuse decline.

Circle four: Stewardship of creation. When people are reconciled with one another, they work together to improve their environment. As a result, artistic expression flourishes (e.g., school children paint murals for their public schools). In addition, people are less likely to use resources selfishly, thus pollution is reduced for a better and more wholesome environment.[11]

Key Indicators of a Transformed City

What would a city look like that has been transformed by Jesus Christ and his kingdom values?

Christian Direction has chosen these 12 indicators for the cities of Québec and La Francophonie that inspire our vision for a transformed city.

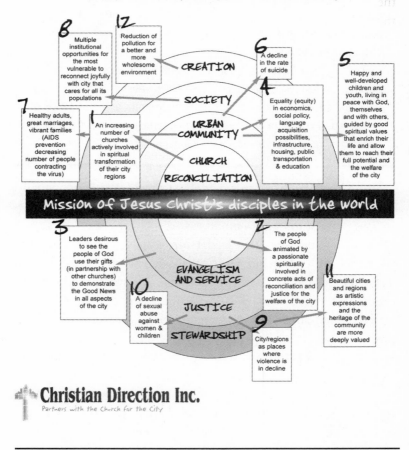

8 Multiple institutional opportunities for the most vulnerable to reconnect joyfully with city that cares for all its populations

12 Reduction of pollution for a better and more wholesome environment

CREATION

6 A decline in the rate of suicide

SOCIETY

4 Equality (equity) in economics, social policy, language acquisition possibilities, infrastructure, housing, public transportation & education

URBAN COMMUNITY

5 Happy and well-developed children and youth, living in peace with God, themselves and with others, guided by good spiritual values that enrich their life and allow them to reach their full potential and the welfare of the city

7 Healthy adults, great marriages, vibrant families (AIDS prevention decreasing number of people contracting the virus)

1 An increasing number of churches actively involved in spiritual transformation of their city regions

CHURCH

RECONCILIATION

Mission of Jesus Christ's disciples in the world

3 Leaders desirous to see the people of God use their gifts (in partnership with other churches) to demonstrate the Good News in all aspects of the city

2 The people of God animated by a passionate spirituality involved in concrete acts of reconciliation and justice for the welfare of the city

EVANGELISM AND SERVICE

10 A decline of sexual abuse against women & children

JUSTICE

11 Beautiful cities and regions as artistic expressions and the heritage of the community are more deeply valued

STEWARDSHIP

9 City/regions as places where violence is in decline

Christian Direction Inc.
Partners with the Church for the City

Figure 5.1.

WHAT WOULD SHALOM LOOK LIKE IN ANY CITY?

Urban peace and well-being characterize a kind of city that pursues fundamental changes, a stable future and the sustaining and enhancing of all of life rooted in a vision bigger than mere urban politics. It is an open-ended, multilayered process, at once social and personal, that is energized by hope yet rooted in the struggles of the present.

The twelve indicators are our best contextual response to issues *of* the city, not just issues *in* the city. This vision seeks to help congregations and social service agencies participate in the transformation of the city, particularly in an era of broken relationships and the holistic understanding of poverty, which sees it as fundamentally relational.

Smith has introduced this model in Canada, Haiti and globally. Its success is due to the emphasis on the biblical value of peace-making applied to large populations.

Canada. Under Smith's leadership, Christian Direction has partnered with churches and social agencies to create shalom through a variety of community development programs: Accroche Youth Centers, Sustainable Urban Community Development, Art with the Most Vulnerable, Partners in the Marketplace, Protestant Partnership on Education, and Ministry in Culture.[12]

Haiti. After his first trip to Haiti in 1979, Smith went back for an internship during his doctoral studies in 1990. He returned again in 1995 to teach, and in 1999 he lived there. Since 1995 Smith has trained twelve hundred urban practitioners and has developed five city networks. In 2000 he received an honorary doctorate from the Union of Private Universities.

The January 12, 2010, earthquake and its death toll of nearly a quarter of a million people created enormous need. The capital of Port-au-Prince experienced a complete disintegration of property, financial and birth records. More than a year later over one million people were still living in makeshift tents. Smith's efforts have created a foundation upon which many partners are able to build. He has developed leader networks in Port-au-Prince, Petionville, Gonaïves, Limbé and Cap Haitian. Within those networks Smith and his team have trained posttrauma and grief counselors.

Lausanne. Smith succeeded Ray Bakke as the senior urban associate of Lausanne, and for two-and-a-half years he served as editor of *World Pulse,* the monthly online magazine of Lausanne. He has served as a coach and mentor for Lausanne's urban ministry leaders for more than twenty-five years.

His role for Cape Town 2010 was to oversee the afternoon seminars. The complexity of this task was remarkable considering the multiple languages spoken and the number of presenters. The seminar topics ranged from the secularism of Europe and North America to the persecution of the church in Asia and the Middle East.

CHRISTIAN DIRECTION

By mobilizing churches and training lay people to engage communities, Christian Direction

- *makes it possible for twelve hundred children to participate in a stay-in-school program in three boroughs of Montréal;*
- *engages three hundred marketplace leaders in twenty-seven weekly Bible studies;*
- *provides a breadth of services that include language acquisition, youth centers for dropout youth, artistic seminars to engage vulnerable people and theological training in multiple languages;*
- *equips local leaders and congregations to determine the success of neighborhood schools, to analyze food security and to provide opportunities for microenterprise.*

WHAT WOULD SHALOM LOOK LIKE IN HAITI?

Any discussion about shalom in Haiti must be within the historical context. The island of Hispanola was divided in 1697. This began the first of four "globalizations." First there was the globalization of colonial exploration that decimated the indigenous population. Then came the globalization of the sugar trade that included the slave trade and its horrible results on the country. Then came the globalization of imperial power and the struggle for political control. The final globalization is that of free trade, which includes the drug trade that dominates the economics of Haiti. This affects the social imaginary[13] of its citizens.

To understand the essence of the worldview of Haitians, it is critical to grasp how the volatile mix of superstition, fatalism, paternalism, population explosion, illiteracy, malnutrition and AIDS is affecting this people. Furthermore, voodoo runs through the nation's total economic and social framework. This dialectic goes on between the poor (who are taxed by superstitions and voodoo practices) and the dominant classes (who use this belief system to oppress the poor). Everything from "spells" on the tap-tap (taxi) to protect it, to participation in the national lottery (three per day), provides a lens on living in Haiti.

I like the indicators that networks of congregations in eight cities have created. Christians are working toward a future where people have true choices. Essentially, poverty is about relationships. It is not just about economics. Poverty is a broad concept that involves economic, social, emotional, physical and spiritual realities. It is often intergenerational. It affects people's identity (social exclusion, absence of harmony in life and well-being) and their vocation (deprivation at every level of life including one's ability to participate in the welfare of the community). The causes of poverty can be traced to "inadequacies in the worldview," which are in fact a web of lies beyond the mere cognitive level of deception. This intricate web leads people to believe that their poverty or social status is somehow divinely sanctioned or a factor of fate. People sense that they have no choices. The social imaginary is a powerful instrument in perpetuating chronic poverty; shalom through the Spirit of the resurrected Christ gives people hope!

VISION

As Smith looks to the future, he sees a need for leaders rooted in strong friendships and stable relationships who take their cities and communities seriously. He calls for churches to contextualize their efforts, and he outlines steps any congregation or group can take to launch ministries in their city or region. The tools for transforming a city are simple: a large map, a history book, good shoes, a team to study the region and the ability to follow through on "community development methodology."[14]

Smith sees a new generation of urban ministry practitioners emerging. Targeted outreaches are focusing on the arts, slums, church planting, university ministry and development of prayer movements. He is disturbed, however, by the post-Christendom cultural shift that says no truth is absolute and that all truth must be understood rationally. This kind of thinking, he believes, is what led to the secularization of Europe. Medieval Europe had a stable social order based on divine revelation. After the Enlightenment, however, people came to believe that reality could be understood only rationally. People became increasingly individualistic and isolated. He sees this happening in many Western cities, including Montréal, where 40 percent of people live alone. The decline in Canadian spirituality parallels the declining number of priests in French-speaking Quebec. In 1960, Quebec had 8,400 priests. Today there are fewer than 3,000, and their average age is sixty-three. Religious practices among the general population in Quebec are the lowest on the continent, and only 5 percent attend mass in the urban areas.[15]

In the Northern Hemisphere Smith sees great migration to large cities resulting in rampant racism. Increased spikes in violence indicate that majority-culture people are not responding well to their new neighbors. A second dominant trend in the Northern Hemisphere is the widespread secularism that results in a privatized faith, as evidenced in Montréal and much of the West. Given these trends, Smith says leaders need to be attentive to issues of racism, ethnocentrism and justice.

The Global South, in contrast, shows many encouraging signs of spiritual life in the rapid growth of the church in Africa, Asia and Latin America. Leaders on these three continents are taking urbanism seriously. Given the great issues of poverty in the developing world, urban leadership training is a highly sought resource.[16]

In an interview Glenn Smith quoted F. B. Meyer, who recognized years ago that "Christian missionaries should be strategists, expending their strength where populations teem and rivers of worldwide influence have their rise."

Smith advises leaders of all continents to go deep into the issues of the soul to develop the strength to resist becoming impatient, lustful or immoral—temptations that are common to aging leaders. The need for a dynamic presence of God's Spirit in the life of the leader is paramount. The best evangelistic witness is people who love their families. In a context of increasing brokenness, whole and spiritually vibrant families will attract people to faith.

Smith practices what he preaches about relationships. In addition to Ray Bakke, who gave Smith a love for the city, other friends who shaped Smith's thinking and help to keep his ministry focused are Keith Price, his exegetical professor, who gave him a love for the Bible; Wilf White, his local pastor, who gave Smith a

HOW DO FRIENDSHIPS AFFECT SHALOM IN YOUR LIFE AND IN YOUR CITY?

Six men have been a part of my journey for twenty to thirty years. Those of us who live in Montréal meet every other week. We meet with the others two to three times a year. Peace and well-being in our lives, our marriages, with our children, in our vocations and our cities dominate the rambling conversations, Bible studies, book readings and especially the arguments! These men love me and care for me.

For us, urban discipleship and shalom mean getting serious about issues like good schools, responsible government, sanitation and clean streets, fairness in the marketplace and justice in the courts. It means working to eliminate squalor slums and every depressing condition that dishonors God by degrading human life. As we see the big picture of what it means to be citizens of the kingdom in the cities as they are, we are free to begin to work from a new and enlarged perspective. Obedience to Jesus takes us to every nook and cranny of city life. We find the challenges innumerable and the cost often high. But we know that while the dark powers are awesome, God's rule is greater and its advance is worth every sacrifice!

---

love for the church; Gordon MacDonald, pastor and author, who meets with Smith three times a year; and Don Posterski, a fellow national leader in Canada who gave Smith a love of culture.

Just as Smith calls leaders to develop loving relationships with family and friends, he urges them to do the same with their cities. Smith calls leaders to love their cities. He challenges them to study the culture and to discern the worldview of people who populate their neighborhoods. He quotes William Booth in asking the question: "Can we weep for them? If you can't weep, we cannot use you." Smith is working to raise up leaders who love their cities enough to weep for them.

Smith echoes Dietrich Bonhoeffer's warning of what happens when the church sells out to the culture. The privatization of faith and individualism neuters the church and prevents it from being a force for good in the community. When churches are reconciled *to* one another rather than isolated *from* one another, they have the most potential for good.

LEADER APPLICATION

- What vocational or ministry network can you join or start in your city?
- What steps can you take to identify or deepen your personal spiritual and relational foundations?

A prayer . . .

Jesus,

Help me to identify leaders in my community who share my passion for my city. Build deep friendships among us so that together we can transform our communities.

GLENN SMITH'S MAJOR LIFE EVENTS

1974	Becomes a university chaplain
1979	First trip to Haiti
1983	Becomes executive director of Christian Direction in Montréal
1987	Attends Young Leaders Congress in Singapore
1989	Works with Ray Bakke to begin Urban Leader Network
1990	Studies in Haiti
1991-1993	Has special assignment in Montréal with Provincial Government
1995	Begins teaching 1,200 urban practitioners in Haiti
1999	Lives in Haiti during a sabbatical

2000	Receives honorary doctorate in Haiti
2004	Appointed as senior associate for urban mission and facilitator for all senior associates for the Lausanne Movement
2010	Coordinates multiplex discussions and dialogue sessions for 4,100 delegates from 203 nations at Lausanne in Cape Town

Richard Stearns

RESCUE

A Heart Aligned with God

LEARN: Surrender your skills and training to rescue those closest to God's heart—the widow and the orphan.

SUCCEED: Be willing to "bet the farm" on God.

When World Vision wanted to connect with churches in the New York City area, they asked for my help. "We are doing great work all over the world," said Scott Jackson, vice president. "But in the United States we have made every mistake possible. You can save us ten years in figuring out what to do in New York."

I was more than happy to share what I had learned, so I met with World Vision leaders in March 2001 at the World Vision office in Seattle. When I met with Rich Stearns, he took the conversation in a different direction and asked me a question I wasn't expecting. "What can I do to help your organization?" he asked. Although I was surprised by the question, I recognized the opportunity and answered without hesitation. "We're having our first public event on September 21 in Manhattan," I said. "Would you invite Bill Hybels to come and speak?"

Hybels was and still is the pastor of Willow Creek Community Church, perhaps the most influential church in America, and he had served on the World Vision board of directors.

"I will ask," Stearns said, "but he doesn't even speak for us!"

As promised, Stearns sent the invitation to Hybels. It landed on his desk a short time before Stearns and two previous World Vision presidents were scheduled to speak at Willow Creek.

Even though Concerts of Prayer Greater New York (COPGNY) was virtually unknown at the time, Hybels accepted the invitation. "World Vision is doing this for me," Hybels responded, "so I will do this for them."

As it turned out, the question Stearns asked me changed the trajectory of World Vision's involvement in New York City.

Rich Stearns and Bill Hybels arrived in New York on September 21, 2001, ten days after 9/11. It was a powerful moment for New York City church leaders to see these two prominent leaders ten days after the worst tragedy in the city's history. During that time, World Vision and COPGNY created the American Families Assistance Fund, which raised six million dollars. The funds were distributed largely through local churches to assist victims of 9/11.

DEFINING MOMENTS

Rich Stearns came to Christ as a result of his future wife's witness. Stearns had lumped Christianity together with Santa Claus and the Easter Bunny, so he didn't take Reneé or her faith seriously when they met at Cornell University. She persisted in her witness, however, and gave Stearns a copy of *Basic Christianity* by John R. W. Stott.

By the time Stearns got around to reading the book, he was in graduate school at Wharton School of Management. He picked up the book on a Saturday night and couldn't put it down. He read until four in the morning as the truth of God came crashing into his life. Stearns and Reneé were married in June 1975. She would finish her bachelor of arts degree in government at Cornell University and receive a law degree from Boston College.

He found more books on the subject and continued to read. Months later, after reading the Bible and fifty other books, Stearns was convinced of Christ's reality. He realized the implications for his life, accepted the weightiness of this commitment and surrendered to Christ. Stearns described his conversion as "betting the farm"—there was no turning back.[1]

Several years after earning his M.B.A, Stearns began work at Parker Brothers and became president in 1984 at age thirty-three. He lost this job due to a change in ownership. He became vice president at Franklin Mint in 1985, but was fired after nine months.

The next fourteen months of unemployment turned into a crisis of faith for Stearns. He realized that God was teaching him something, but what? What did God want him to learn about career and calling? Stearns was learning a new level of brokenness and dependence on God. As a former CEO, he was used to making the decisions and calling the shots. His wilderness experience of unemployment put an important spiritual stake in the ground. God addressed Stearns's priorities to get him headed in the right direction. During this season of seeing God at work in bringing him to deeper levels of surrender, Stearns landed a position at Lenox in 1987 as president of Lenox Collections. In 1995, Stearns was named president and chief executive officer of Lenox Inc., overseeing three divisions, six manufacturing facilities, four thousand employees and $500 million in annual sales.

Years later he discovered this insight in a book by John Ortberg: "For many people, a career becomes the altar on which they sacrifice their lives. . . . A calling, which is something I do for God, is replaced by a career, which threatens to become my god."[2]

In 1997, after leading Lenox for nine years, Stearns received a phone call from Bill Bryce, a long-time development staff member with World Vision. Bob Seiple, World Vision president, had announced his intentions to step down. When Bryce got Stearns on the phone, he said, "Since I first heard of Bob's decision a couple of weeks ago, I've been praying that God would lead the right person to take his place. Don't ask me to explain it, but God told me that you are going to be the next president of World Vision."[3]

Stearns was stunned. He had a great job. Heading up a not-for-profit organization, even one as large as World Vision, was not part of his life plan. Despite his reluctance, Stearns participated in the interview process out of respect for Bill Bryce and World Vision. After months of correspondence, interviews and a final two-day meeting with the World Vision board, he was asked to take the position. Stearns had to make a decision.

In his book *The Hole in Our Gospel,* he describes his emotional state during this time:

> Would I accept the board's invitation, leave my twenty-three-year career behind, and move my wife and five kids across the country, or would I turn down the job and stay at Lenox? . . . I was afraid. . . . I was an emotional basket case. And so, at 4 p.m., I slipped into my pajamas, crawled into bed, pulled the covers over my head, and began to weep and pray, crying out to God to "take this cup" from me. It was pretty pathetic. Andy, sixteen at the time, came into my room a few minutes later, patted me on the shoulder, and said, "Everything will be okay, Dad. . . ." There I was, blubbering in front of my teenager—quite the spiritual role model![4]

After reading the story of the rich young ruler in Matthew 19, Stearns realized that Jesus wanted everything from him, which included a willingness to move across the country and to give up the high-paying job. Stearns surrendered and said yes to God.

CONSEQUENTIAL IMPACT

When Stearns took the World Vision position, he was betting the farm again—this time professionally. He made the decision to leave the posh corner office of a successful corporation to become CEO of a faith-based charity. This was a remarkable journey for a person who grew up in a one-parent household in which the family was one paycheck away from being broke. After working hard to escape the life of the "have-nots" to become one of the "haves," he was choosing to give up much of what he had gained to become an advocate for those still stuck in poverty. The table below expresses the mind-bending income gap between people living in the United States and those living in the grip of deep poverty.

Table 6.1

The Haves and the Have-Nots		
Earning less than $2 a day	2.6 billion people	40 percent of the world's people
Earning less than $1 a day	1.0 billion people	15 percent of the world's people
Earning $105 a day (USA)	0.3 billion people	4.5 percent of the world's people

Source: Stearns, *Hole in Our Gospel*, p. 122.

Stearns often challenges leaders by asking them the question: "What does betting the farm mean for you? Is it your career, your income, comfortable home, community where you live, or even the little things that pull you away from the commitment to the Lord? Ask yourself the same questions that Jesus asked the rich young ruler, and if you can't answer them with an unconditional 'Yes,' then you probably have some work to do with God."[5]

Under Stearns's leadership, World Vision has reached three important objectives: (1) recommitting to its Christian identity; (2) taking on HIV/AIDS as a call to engage the church; (3) strengthening the company by establishing best business practices, creating a culture of excellence and seeing the revenue tripled to over one billion dollars annually.

Recommitting to Christian identity. When Stearns started working for World Vision in 1998, the relief agency was facing significant internal challenges. "World Vision was a solid organization, but it had begun to drift," Stearns says. "World Vision had been far more reliant on its mass marketing strategies using television than on having an intentional strategy to engage the church. We were in danger of drifting toward secularism. We lacked a culture of accountability. Our ratio of overhead costs to ministry costs was unacceptably high."[6]

Furthermore, church engagement was negligible. Fewer than three thousand children were being sponsored by churches in the United States annually when Stearns joined World Vision.

Stearns is a careful student of Scripture, and through his time in Bible study and church involvement he came to some crucial conclusions about the importance of the church. These conclusions resulted in significant changes at World Vision. Stearns issued a prophetic call to them to reengage the church, to be a part of the church, not just a parachurch organization. In the same way that the disciples took care of the widows in the first century (Acts 6), Stearns sees World Vision as an expression of the church on special assignment to the poor.

When I asked Stearns to describe his passion for the church in America, he said, "The church has to lead the way on global poverty. We are the body of Christ, and I believe that this is our assignment together."

Today, thirteen years later, as many as fifteen thousand child sponsors are being recruited annually from local churches.[7] Globally more than four million children are sponsored through World Vision in more than fifty countries. Nearly 50 percent of all sponsored children today live in communities severely affected by HIV/AIDS.

Taking on HIV/AIDS as a call to engage the church. Stearns was an early observer of the crisis of HIV and AIDS in Africa. The pan-

demic began in the early 1980s in Southern Uganda. In the 1980s
and '90s the discussion of HIV/AIDS became part of the culture
wars because the disease was associated with homosexuality. "Less
than 3 percent of church attendees surveyed said they would
support a child orphaned by HIV/AIDS," Stearns explained. "Stig-
matization was that bad." One Christian school principal asked
him if "everybody in Africa was gay."[8]

As the pandemic raged, 250,000 people were dying monthly,
leaving behind six thousand orphans every day. As Princess Zulu
of Zambia, a spokesperson for World Vision and a carrier of HIV/
AIDS, so eloquently says, "There are 10,000 African villages
sobbing every night."[9]

Stearns decided to take a stand. He made his first trip to Rakai,
Uganda—"ground zero" of the AIDS pandemic—in 1998. He describes his encounter with a child named Richard.

> I sat inside his meager thatch hut, listening to his story, told
> through the tears of an orphan whose parents had died of
> AIDS. At thirteen, Richard was trying to raise his two younger
> brothers by himself in this small shack with no running water,
> electricity, or even beds to sleep in. There are no adults in their
> lives—no one to care for them, feed them, love them, or teach
> them how to become men. There was no one to hug them
> either, or to tuck them in at night. Other than his siblings,
> Richard was alone, as no child should be. . . .
>
>   I didn't want to be there. I had to see and smell and touch
> the pain of the poor.[10]

Stearns describes the emotions he felt after returning from
Uganda. "I was both heartbroken and angry that the world was
not doing enough to help."[11] But an even bigger question was,
"Where was the church?"[12]

Stearns's leadership is characterized by the principle "Cast and
live your vision." He cast the vision for the church to be the pro-

phetic voice to care for widows and orphans. Then he embodied the vision by implementing the change to make it happen. Stearns took trips to the most desperate corners of the planet—including East Africa, South Africa and India. His leadership has generated remarkable, tangible results.[13]

Stearns summarizes the horrific reality of HIV/AIDS with these statistics (as of 2008):

- More than 33 million people are infected; 70 percent of those live in Africa.

- More than 25 million have died of HIV/AIDS since 1981.

- Three nations in sub-Saharan Africa have an infection rate of over 20 percent (Swaziland, Botswana and Lesotho).

- According to the CIA *World Factbook,* nine nations have an infection rate of more than 10 percent.

- India is the second largest region in the world affected by HIV/AIDS.

- 15 million children are now orphaned by HIV/AIDS.[14]

But statistics do not convey the emotional, spiritual, mental and financial devastation. Stearns believes that the urgency of the AIDS crisis is an opportunity for the U.S. church to save lives and combat poverty.

In New York City on September 21, 2001, Stearns delivered his "One Hundred Crashing Airliners" speech. What would it be like, he asked, if on a single day one hundred airplanes crashed, filled with children under the age of five? Because that's how many children die each day of preventable causes. Imagine the global media coverage. What if that happened two or three days in a row? Imagine the frenzy that would follow. Using the crashing-airplane comparison, Stearns pleaded with churches to accept the moral obligation to take on the challenge of child mortality, which would include HIV/AIDS.

Stearns returned from Africa convinced that World Vision could and should accept the challenge to take hope and help to those dying alone in unimaginable conditions. But he faced a challenge. "I was asking World Vision, a G-rated ministry, to take on an R-rated issue," says Stearns. "Leaders in our marketing department thought this could be organizationally crippling to be aligned with a disease associated with the homosexual community."[15]

But Stearns was convincing. The entire leadership of World Vision, from the board to the marketing team, was convinced that this was the right direction to move.

The Hope Initiative was launched in 2002 with a tour and an HIV forum. The meetings were led by senior World Vision spokespersons who went to Washington, D.C., and New York City. Their message energized churches. Also in 2002 Stearns accompanied Tommy Thompson, Secretary of Health and Human Services, on a visit to four African nations with soaring HIV infection rates. This laid important groundwork for President Bush's AIDS initiative.

Four million AIDS patients in Africa required anti-retroviral drugs to stay alive; fewer than fifty thousand were receiving them. For twenty-five dollars a month,[16] America could extend an AIDS patient's life for years. Motivated by these numbers, President Bush proposed legislation to support the work of AIDS relief in Africa. The legislation was called PEPFAR—President's Emergency Plan for AIDS Relief.

The plan established three objectives: (1) treat two million AIDS patients; (2) prevent seven million new infections; (3) care for ten million HIV-infected people.

The proposed fifteen-billion-dollar legislation was approved in the House of Representatives by a vote of 375 to 41 in the spring of 2003.[17] World Vision played an instrumental role in drafting the language for this legislation.

Through the work of World Vision in Africa, in 2005:

- 895,000 children received HIV prevention training;

- 59,000 home visits provided care for orphans, vulnerable children and chronically ill persons as part of 3,700 community care coalitions;

- 842,000 orphans and vulnerable children received some form of care;

- 69,000 chronically ill persons received home-based care;

- 418 programs engaged in some form of district-level, HIV-related advocacy; and

- 54,000 people, including 10,000 senior faith leaders from 8,100 congregations, participated in HIV and AIDS church mobilization activities.[18]

World Vision also has become the leading American voice on behalf of the orphans and widows devastated by HIV and AIDS, especially in East and Southern Africa. In Rwanda, thousands of children have shoes to wear and have begun to attend school because New York City churches are their sponsors. "In Zambia ten years ago everyone was dying," says Stearns. "Today people are living functional, healthy lives as the incidences have dropped, medicines have become available and the orphan crisis has abated. Today, in many places, the pandemic is being managed, allowing people to live longer."[19]

Strengthening World Vision. In thirteen years at the helm of World Vision U.S. (1998-2011), Rich Stearns tripled the income (from 350 million dollars to more than 1 billion dollars per year) and reduced the overhead by one third (from 21 to 14 percent).

Table 6.2 demonstrates the growth of World Vision U.S. under Stearns's leadership: a 292 percent growth in annual income and an 88.5 percent increase in the number of children sponsored from the U.S. World Vision office.[20] In addition to tripling the income of the organization, World Vision has been able to attract in-kind resources from U.S. government agencies such as USAID in the form of foodstuffs. Larry Probus, chief financial officer, explains in a 2011 video how every $1 invested in child sponsorship attracts $1.50 in benefits.[21] The organizational excellence of World Vision has become a best practice learned over sixty years in the long-term sustainable community development. Stearns has said, "Addressing poverty is rocket science—in addressing all of the complex issues which comprise poverty."

Table 6.2

Year	Income	Child Sponsorships
1998	$356 million	565,000
1999	$407 million	577,000
2000	$469 million	669,000
2001	$525 million	670,000
2002	$553 million	735,000
2003	$686 million	733,000
2004	$807 million	776,000
2005	$905 million	812,000
2006	$944 million	851,000
2007	$957 million	921,000
2008	$1.11 billion	1,004,000
2009	$1.22 billion	1,016,000
2010	$1.04 billion	1,067,000

VISION

Stearns speaks candidly about the progress made as well as the desperate needs not yet met. "I am proud of what World Vision has achieved, but we are only a pea shooter trying to bring down an elephant," he says. "There are still two billion people living in desperate poverty on less than two dollars per day. World Vision's annual global revenues of 2.7 billion dollars is equal to only a few days' sales for Walmart."[22]

He believes that American churches, the wealthiest in history, have the resources to tackle global poverty. "The Christians who attend the 340,000 churches in the United States control 5.2 trillion dollars of wealth," Stearns says. "If everyone in the local church simply tithed—American Christians give only 2.4 percent of their incomes—we could bring global poverty to a manageable level."[23]

This could end what Bono, humanitarian and lead singer of the rock band U2, calls "stupid poverty," a phrase that describes situations in which children die of diseases that a twenty-cent immunization could prevent. If properly allocated, the resources and technology we have available could make this happen.

Stearns envisions World Vision and its partners, over the next five years, reaching ten million more children in sixteen countries. He will continue to challenge more and more American Christians to "bet the farm" of their personal wealth to serve the poorest of the poor. "I challenge people to do something risky, reckless and costly," Stearns says. "We should give in such a way that we find ourselves waking up in a cold sweat wondering how we will cover the commitment." Stearns quotes World Vision founder Bob Pierce: "Leadership sticks its neck out—pushing to the edge, leaving room for God to act."[24]

Stearns challenges leaders to fully grasp God's kingdom. As evidence that the kingdom is here now, Stearns recounts the story of Luke 7. When asked by the disciples of John the Baptist if Jesus is the One to come, Jesus answers by alluding to Isaiah 61:1, where good news is preached to the poor: "[Tell John that] the blind receive sight, the lame walk, those who have leprosy are cleansed, the deaf hear, the dead are raised, and the good news is proclaimed to the poor" (Luke 7:22; Isaiah 61).

Stearns wants to be like Oskar Schindler, the man who saved more than one thousand Jewish people in World War II from extermination by hiring them to work in his German factory and protecting them. He describes Schindler's tearful reaction after realizing he could have sold his gold ring to save one more person. Stearns said, "I want to be like Schindler. I want to do everything I know to do to save just one more."[25]

LEADER APPLICATION

- What would complete surrender to God look like for you? What might God be asking you to re-evaluate (e.g., career, location, income, future)?

- What radical step would you be willing to take in the next twelve months to free up more time or resources to make a difference in the lives of the desperately poor (e.g., lifestyle, travel, local engagement)?

A prayer . . .

Jesus,

Align my life with your concern for the poor. Help me to live with open hands and surrendered heart so that I can engage your larger concerns.

RICHARD STEARNS'S MAJOR LIFE EVENTS

1977	Named president of Parker Brothers
1985	Named president of Franklin Mint
1987	Named president of Lenox
1998	Named president of World Vision United States
2002	Launches Hope Initiative with World Vision resulting in tens of thousands of sponsored children
2009	World Vision influences PEPFAR legislation resulting in $15 billion in funding for HIV-affected countries; *The Hole in Our Gospel* is published by Thomas Nelson
2010	*The Hole in Our Gospel* is named the 2010 Christian Book of the Year by the Evangelical Christian Publishers Association; it is one of the best handbooks on global poverty

Ajith Fernando

SUFFERING

Lessons from the Suffering Church in Asia

LEARN: To identify with the poor through suffering
is a way of incarnating the gospel.

SUCCEED: Be willing to cross religious, ethnic, racial and
socioeconomic boundaries to reach people.

When I met Ajith Fernando he was leading the Bible exposition at the 1993 Urbana Missions Conference. Since then I have heard Fernando speak in several other contexts, including Cape Town 2010, where he taught from the book of Ephesians.

In his exposition of chapter 1, Fernando spoke about the centrality of Christ's suffering as God's redemptive act. He spoke about the grandness of God's salvation and its cosmic nature. "I have worked with first-generation Christians for thirty-four years," Fernando said. "People come to Christ to meet a personal need. They stay with Christ because he is the truth."[1] The truth about God is that he won the world through the suffering of his Son.

In 2008 I met Ajith's brother Priyan, an executive vice president for American Express in Manhattan. We met through a mutual friend, Heather Atria, who runs American Express's Christian Network (SALT).[2] When Priyan and I met in his office near the World Trade Center, I learned that he is the brother of Ajith.

After that meeting, Priyan became a board member of our organization, the New York City Leadership Center, and in 2009 he

WHAT IS IT LIKE TO WORK WITH FIRST-GENERATION CHRISTIANS IN A CONTEXT OF POVERTY, AND WHAT IS THE REWARD?

When those we minister to are sick, they expect us to come and visit. Visiting is a wonderful trait of poor people. They visit those who are in need. And if we do not go, because we are simply too busy or out of town, they blame us. A small price to pay in a glorious ministry! This has been a challenge to us now that my wife is down with cancer. The church members want to visit her. And we tell them not to come. Some come anyway. Some may stay for as long as four hours. It is very tiring for my wife who is going through chemotherapy. But most do not come. They are very poor. But every Sunday I come back from church with parcels of fruits, vegetables, soups and other things that the members have heard are good for cancer patients: gifts joyfully and sacrificially given by very poor people.

What is the reward? I guess the greatest is the joy of seeing people who should otherwise be dead, or in prison or leading underworld gangs, serving God as YFC [Youth for Christ] staff, doing the kind of ministry I could never do. In addition they are good biblical preachers too. What a joy to know that people I could not otherwise come into contact with, are now my sons in the faith; people who are close friends and from whom I learn so much about the world I was insulated from as a child.

invited my wife, Marya, and me to his New Jersey home to have dinner with Ajith and his wife, Nelun. As Ajith and I spoke that night I was impressed by the passion of his intellect and the joyfulness of his demeanor. I was reminded once again that people who have seen much suffering have a refreshing appreciation for the goodness of God.

The context of Fernando's thirty-five years of leadership has been his homeland, Sri Lanka, an island-nation that is the strategic naval link between West Asia and Southeast Asia.[3] The country became independent from the United Kingdom in 1948 after more than 150 years of British rule. Less than forty years after gaining independence, however, the country ended up in a twenty-six-year civil war (1983-2009). One of the minorities, the Tamils (often referred to as Tamil Tigers or Liberation Tigers), led a separation movement, using terrorism to disrupt civic life.[4] Most of Fernando's ministry was during these years of danger and unrest.

Table 7.1

Sri Lanka's Ethnic Communities	
Sinhalese	74 percent
Tamil	13 percent
Moors	7 percent

Table 7.2

Sri Lanka's Religious Communities	
Buddhist	70 percent
Hindu	15 percent
Muslim	8 percent
Christian	8 percent
Roman Catholic	6 percent
Protestant Evangelical	2 percent

Source: "Sri Lanka," in *The Cambridge FactFinder*, ed. David Crystal, 4th ed. (Cambridge: Cambridge University Press, 2000), p. 331.

Sri Lanka's Buddhist history dates back to the second century. It was the first Buddhist nation to send missionaries.[5] Today Sri Lanka's twenty million citizens live in nine provinces,[6] and they live on less than six dollars per day, with a GDP per capita of $2,000 per year.[7] Tables 7.1 and 7.2, respectively, outline the primary ethnic and religious communities in the nation.

Marya's and my affection for the South Asian Christian community dates back to 1983 when we lived for ten weeks in Bihar, India, just below Nepal. Bihar is the size of Nebraska but has a population of more than 100 million people. It is the birthplace of Buddhism and a stronghold of militant Hinduism and Islam. The ratio of Hindus and Muslims to Christians is 100,000 to 1. We were close enough to Sri Lanka, which is just off of the southeast tip of India, that we could hear Sri Lankan radio programs.

DEFINING MOMENTS

Fernando's father, Benjamin Edward Fernando, was a fourth-generation Christian in Sri Lanka. His mother was a convert to Christianity from Buddhism.

During Fernando's childhood years, corruption was tolerated, even expected in Sri Lanka. But Fernando's father was extremely conscientious in his job as commissioner of internal revenue. "He did not allow any bribery or corruption within his sphere of influence," Fernando told me. When his father reached the retirement age of fifty-five, he expected to receive an employment extension, which was normal practice, but it was denied. "He had alienated his superiors because he would not participate in corruption."[8]

Soon after losing his job, his father was offered a position with World Vision. He left his family and lived among the poor of Bangladesh for the next few years. He was one of the pioneers in using village development committees to administer the aid given by World Vision. He returned home and founded World Vision Sri

Lanka, where he worked from 1977 to 1989. His years of working for World Vision were among the best of his career.

"We had people in our home at all times of the day," says Fernando's brother Priyan. "My mother kept our home sane in the way that she nurtured us spiritually. She was a very godly influence on all of my siblings."[9] Ajith and his older brother, Duleep, became preachers. Priyan is a businessman, and another brother became a medical doctor who has worked among the poor in Sri Lanka for twenty-five years.

Ajith Fernando was converted at the age of fourteen, primarily through his mother's influence. Shortly after this he sensed a call to be a preacher and to work with the poor.

"Every week I would write a sermon and mail it to a friend who did not have a church nearby," he explains. "At times the need to preach became so intense that I would go down to the beach and preach to the ocean. I also wanted to identify with the poor so badly that I would sleep on the floor for a few weeks."[10]

At the age of sixteen, Fernando became involved with Youth for Christ and was mentored by Sam Sherrard, who had been influenced by Robert Coleman's *The Master Plan of Evangelism*. Under Sherrard's influence Fernando developed a deep burden to take the gospel to outsiders. Every Sunday he met with Sam and other YFC volunteers from nine until after midnight.

Buddhism was prevalent in all aspects of life in Sri Lanka. When Fernando entered college, he was the only Protestant in the school of science. He had to wrestle with the implications of his Christian faith within the context of strong nationalism that saw Christianity as a foreign religion.

Fernando's father, as chairman of the Bible Society board, got to know American Christian leaders Paul Rees and Carl Henry during their trips to Asia. Rees headed the World Vision pastors' conferences sponsored by the Bible Society movement. Henry, a giant in the modern evangelical movement in the United States, was a cofounder of *Christianity Today* and author of *The Uneasy Conscience of Modern Fundamentalism*. Henry was calling the American church to both doctrinal purity and relevant social engagement with the poor. Rees and Henry opened doors for Ajith to get scholarships to study in the United States. While he was in the U.S., both men had a great influence on him not only through their books but also through their personal correspondence and care for him.[11]

Henry's influence can be seen in Fernando's writing: "The most serious blind spot in the Asian church is the view that God is love and does not require any personal accountability for our actions. The most serious blind spot in the West is a defective understanding of suffering."[12]

At Asbury Seminary, Fernando was able to study under Robert Coleman, who encouraged him to develop a simple lifestyle. "He never took any money for his books. I have never taken any money for my books either," Fernando says. "The entire honorarium I receive goes to my organization."[13] Fernando also studied under Robert Traina, the father of inductive Bible study, the method that helped shape InterVarsity Christian Fellowship's Bible and Life curriculum.

As a young man, Fernando devoured John Stott's Bible expositions that he read from the Urbana Missions Conference Compendiums in his father's library. These gave him a taste of Bible exposition. In subsequent years he did the Bible expositions at four Urbana conferences.

The teaching of John Seamands on the "glory of Asian cultures" was pivotal in determining Fernando's worldview and vision. As a follower of a minority religion influenced by the British understanding of culture, Fernando struggled to appreciate the God-given uniqueness of his culture. Thanks to Seamands, Fernando learned to celebrate his Asian origin rather than be ashamed of it.

CONSEQUENTIAL IMPACT

Desiring to identify with his suffering people, Fernando returned to Sri Lanka at age twenty-seven and began his term as president of Youth for Christ. He knew that returning to Sri Lanka would involve suffering and deprivation. He also believed, however, that "the happiest people in the world are those unafraid of suffering."[14] With a commitment to live simply and to identify with his people, Fernando led Youth for Christ for thirty-five years in his poor, war-torn, religiously hostile homeland.

After attending an Urbana Missions Conference in the U.S. in 1987, Fernando helped start three Urbana-type conferences in Sri Lanka. These events helped mobilize a new generation of evangelists. Fernando and his teams were committed to reach the poor and the semiliterate. Over the next thirty years approximately 50 percent of all conversions were of people from other faiths. The following decades of evangelism happened during the period of the civil war (1983-2009) in which many people died. According to one estimate, between 80,000 and 100,000 people were killed in the conflict.[15]

Fernando was also influenced by the movement that arose from the 1974 Lausanne Congress on World Evangelization hosted by Billy Graham. "I went through the Lausanne booklet *Gospel and Culture* paragraph by paragraph with our staff, and we applied everything it taught into our context," he said. "The covenant that came out of the Lausanne conference presented the relationship between evangelism and social concern in a fresh and powerful way."[16]

When Fernando took over as president in 1975, Youth for Christ Sri Lanka had eight staff. Today there are eighty staff and five hundred volunteers. Despite the financial limitations, danger and religiously hostile environment, the organization expanded ten times in thirty-five years under Fernando's leadership.

Suffering among the poor. The strategy for reaching the poor was simple to articulate but not as simple to do. "In working with the poor the need was to live among the poor," Fernando explains.[17] Throughout the years of the civil war, Fernando witnessed much suffering, which has caused him to reflect on the subject. "The Bible often describes suffering as an essential aspect of the Christian life,"[18] he writes. "There are twenty-three different words for joy in the Hebrew Old Testament. I have counted eighteen times where suffering and joy are mentioned together. And often the suffering is given as a reason for the joy."[19]

One of Fernando's great achievements has been his effective endurance through suffering. "We are to 'count' . . . all our trials to be joyful," he writes. "'We know that . . . all things work together for good.' . . . Trials cannot separate us from the love of God."[20]

Fernando sees suffering and martyrdom as God's strategy to grow the church. He quotes sociologist Rodney Stark: "The willingness to suffer in order to care for the sick had a part to play in the large numbers of people in the Roman Empire turning to Christ."[21] The word *martyr* comes from the Greek word for "witness," says Fernando. "To witness is to suffer."[22]

Ministry centers and community development. Youth for Christ flourished under Fernando's leadership. In addition to the increase in staff members, the number of ministry centers increased from 10 in 1976 to 152 in 2011. Ministry centers touched the lives of more than six thousand Sri Lankan youth on a regular basis. The ministry centers provided a place for YFC to host study rooms for students. There is no room for poor children to study in their homes, so the YFC offices were converted to study halls at night.

"We provided a place for supervised study," Fernando said. "In the war zones the students would stay overnight as it was not safe for them to go home. Parents often wanted their children to drop out of school and begin to work at the age of about fourteen. We encouraged young people to stay in school so they could have an education and a future. We also tried to provide scholarship help for the students' basic necessities."[23]

HOW HAS THE THEME OF SUFFERING BEEN WOVEN INTO YOUR OWN CALLING AND EXPERIENCE?

In the providence of God, our calling was to minister to the poor, and most of them were people who had suffered greatly. To identify with such people, we had to adopt a lifestyle that made us accessible to them. One thing that this involved was living a relatively simple life. I wanted our house to be a place where the poor felt at home. So we did not have things which people associate with affluence. We still don't have a microwave oven as such things are strange to our people.

We chose to live on a Sri Lankan salary and not take anything that comes from my overseas speaking and book ministry. That amounts to five to ten times my salary. I guess the thing that we got from this was a happy home. My wife never complained about not having things that others had, and our children seemed to be happy even though they did not have a lot of the things that their relatives had. I do not think that they felt deprived. And in the end, both my children chose to work for the same ministry that I work for.

I guess the hardest part was agonizing with struggling people who, after all the pain that they had experienced, found it difficult to believe that God will look after them. How we yearned to see them have the joy we had. Instead, often they would say things that would hurt us. Hurt people have a way of hurting people! Trying to defend and minister to hurting people often resulted in those they had hurt being upset with us. But we learned not to give up on people who hurt you. We learned to look to the possibilities of grace in hope and long to see these people whole.

Almost all the ministry centers had playgrounds so that poor youth could enjoy sports. During times of war, these were among the only places open that gave the youth a place of hope and fun amid the gloom of living in a war zone.

Youth for Christ pioneered an innovative outreach called Y-Gro. Because of its specialized call to youth evangelism, Youth for Christ could not concentrate on meeting other social needs, so it helped give birth to Y-Gro, which focuses on community development. This group now has a staff of fifty workers.

Surrounded by seemingly insurmountable odds, Fernando has always felt a sense of urgency. He quotes Amy Carmichael, the Irish missionary who cared for children in India for more than fifty years: "We have all eternity to celebrate our victories, but only a few hours before sunset to win them."[24]

Fernando's sense of urgency has led him to innovate. An astute leader, he understands that music is a way of reaching and influencing youth. In the early years of his ministry, the Youth for Christ team studied the culture and the music of young Sri Lankans. Based on their findings, they created new forms of communication to reach young people and adapted their style of music to be more culturally relevant to young people.

Hope for reconciliation. After years of foreign rule and civil war, Sri Lankans have become protective of their cultural identity. In situations like theirs, race and culture become walls that people hide behind. Fernando has discovered that the gospel tears down the dividing walls of culture and race. Youth for Christ was reorganized geographically instead of according to language groups. The new structure allowed Sinhala, Tamil and English-speaking youth to minister together. Although the war is over, the nation is still divided along ethnic lines. Fernando hopes that the YFC example of Sinhala and Tamil youth working together will be a model of hope for ethnic reconciliation in his nation.

Fernando's own family became a metaphor of the healing when his Sinhalese daughter married a man from a Tamil background. The marriage was "a living demonstration of what I had been teaching about racial reconciliation."[25]

International impact. While Fernando built his modest organization in the context of enormous challenges, his international impact grew rapidly. As of 2011, Fernando has spoken in thirty-five countries. He divides his time between speaking in affluent countries and poor countries. "Leaders in poor countries need to be encouraged," he says, and "leaders in affluent countries need to be encouraged and challenged."[26]

Table 7.3

Books by Ajith Fernando	
1985	*Leadership Lifestyle: Study of 1 Timothy*
1987	*The Christian's Attitude Toward World Religions*
1993	*Reclaiming Friendship: Relating to Each Other in a Frenzied World*
1993	*Spiritual Living in a Secular World: Applying the Book of Daniel Today*
1994	*Crucial Questions About Hell*
1998	*Acts* (a commentary)
2001	*Sharing the Truth in Love: The Uniqueness of Christ in an Anything Goes World*
2003	*Jesus Driven Ministry*
2007	*The Fullness of Christ*
2008	*An Authentic Servant: The Marks of a Spiritual Leader*

Fernando has written fifteen books (see table 7.3). The most popular is *Jesus Driven Ministry,* which came about as a result of a request from Leighton Ford in the early 1990s. Ford asked a group of young leaders to choose a passage of Scripture and to jot down what they learned about leadership from Jesus. Fernando chose Mark 1, although he no longer remembers why. "I learned so much that I kept adding material to this study for months to come." The book grew into a fourteen-chapter exposition of Mark 1 and became a handbook for tens of thousands of leaders in many countries around the world.[27] *Jesus Driven Ministry* has been translated into ten languages, including Chinese, Korean, Turkish, Dutch, Spanish and German.

WHAT IS SO IMPORTANT ABOUT WORKING LONG-TERM IN A POOR AND BROKEN NATION?

In 1989 we had just come back to Sri Lanka from a six-month sabbatical at Gordon-Conwell Theological Seminary. It was a workaholic's sabbatical. I learned to use a computer and to type. I almost completed writing two books. I taught a class of graduate students. I preached in the weekends and sometimes mid-week, and through that raised most of the money needed for a colleague to come to the U.S. to do a master's degree. All these things I could not do at home. It was like heaven!

I came back to a country that was going through a revolution. A group of extreme leftist youth in the south were attempting to overthrow the government (this was different from the war raging in the north). All the time, there were bodies floating along the river at the edge of our town. The estimates of how many died that year run as high as 50,000. Almost all were young people.

As a youth worker I struggled with deep discouragement. Schools did not function for months at a time. The rebels had stopped public transport, and most of those in our office traveled to work by bus or train. We needed to pick up our staff from their homes and drop them back. The process took three-and-a-half hours in the morning and the same time in the evening. There were three of us who shared this responsibility. I usually do not enjoy driving, but this time was particularly stressful because most people would give rides to others who were stranded. But if by chance the person we gave a ride to was a rebel, we could all end up dead.

While I was struggling with the sorrow of the situation at home and the frustration of spending most of my time doing what I did not like to do, I got a letter from Gordon-Conwell saying that the faculty had unanimously decided to invite me to join their faculty. The attractiveness of this offer was that ample time was given for writing and for continuing my teaching and preaching ministry. But I knew that was not for me, that I was called for lifetime ministry in Sri Lanka. I especially knew that I could not leave my nation at such a traumatic time. I immediately wrote to say that I am honored by the invitation but that I did not think it was God's will for me.

Youth for Christ gave me a three-month sabbatical beginning in January 2005 to go to the U.S. and work on a book on Deuteronomy that was due at the end of March 2005. A week before I left, the tsunami struck! I assumed that my colleagues could handle the situation and proceeded with my preparation for the trip. About three days after the tsunami, it became clear to me that I could not leave. Possibly 40,000 people had been killed, and there were so many needy people in our country. Our ministry stopped all other work to concentrate on relief for the next four months or so.

I stayed at home, and most of the time I was responding to letters asking about the possibility of funding, and helping match donors with those who could use the funds. Most of our staff workers are not fluent in English, so I had to handle most of the correspondence while they were out in the field ministering to people. I decided that I wouldn't go to sleep until all the letters for the day were answered. Some days I went to sleep at 6.00 a.m. I sometimes wrote as many as 250 letters in a day. I was feeling sorry for myself! I was supposed to be on a sabbatical writing a book on Deuteronomy, and instead I was writing e-mails!

I was asked to speak at the staff prayer meeting on the first day of work for the new year. I prepared a message the night before and went to sleep. When I was praying before going for the meeting, I felt that the message I prepared was not appropriate. So I quickly jotted down notes for another message and went back to praying. Again I felt the message was not suitable. It was time to leave. My daughter was traveling with me in the van, and she asked me what I was going to speak on. Like Abraham told Isaac, I told her, "The Lord will provide a message." As we were nearing the church where we had the meeting, some thoughts began to flow through my mind. When I reached the church I quickly jotted them down and gave that message.

My colleagues told me that I should write that message down. A senior pastor had earlier told me to write something for the pastors who did not know what to tell their people after this terrible tragedy. I wrote it down and sent it to some of my friends by e-mail. A Chinese website asked permission to translate it into Chinese and post it. A Dutch newspaper carried it in their pages. RBC Ministries decided to print it in English, Sinhala and Tamil, doing a total of 100,000 copies, with the name *After the Tsunami*. Then a great earthquake hit Pakistan. The booklet was translated into Urdu with the name *After the Earthquake*. Then came Hurricane Katrina in the U.S. RBC Ministries in the U.S. printed 396,000 copies of this booklet, naming it *After the Hurricane*. A German book and a book by InterVarsity Press USA included it as a chapter in a larger book. Burmese and Japanese editions followed. Many people have written to me that the book was a help to many after the recent tsunami in Japan. RBC's television program decided to follow up the booklet by producing a program for Day of Discovery called "The God of Joy; the God of Pain."

The little message God gave me that day reached well over a million people. And I was complaining about not being able to write! This year I finally sent the manuscript of my Deuteronomy book to the publisher—six years late!

The book illustrates Fernando's ability to teach in a compelling, intellectually challenging way. The book also reveals his philosophy of leadership. He writes, "The greatest crisis facing Christian leadership today concerns lifestyle—always the burning issue." Then he quotes evangelist D. L. Moody, who reportedly said that he had more trouble with himself than with any other person he met![28] The problem with "self," Fernando indicates, is that it's always thinking "me first." Suffering and sacrifice lack magnetic qualities; they attract no one.

VISION

Fernando is committed not only to a national movement among young people and a global teaching ministry, but to his local church and local leaders. In 1979, he discovered a Methodist church where the attendance had dwindled to zero. With his wife and a young couple recently converted in Youth for Christ, he moved to this church and helped bring renewal to it. Today his primary grass-roots ministry is at that church, and about 75 percent of its members are converts from other faiths.

Fernando has mentored more than one hundred Sri Lankan leaders, and he maintains contact with hundreds of young leaders through e-mail. Whenever he has the chance he also spends personal time with these leaders when he is in their countries.[29]

Reflecting on thirty-five years of leadership and world travel, Fernando is concerned about the church in the West. He fears that its portrayal of Christianity as a nice religion but lacking a radical edge will disqualify it from being a respected, missionary-sending body. "Sermons should disturb, convict, and motivate to radical and costly obedience," he says.[30]

Fernando's conviction about the incarnational nature of the gospel empowers him to tear down walls of ethnic identity, to cross barriers of race and socioeconomic differences, and to reach out to people on behalf of Jesus.

LEADER APPLICATION

- What do you need to do to put yourself in a position where you can identify with suffering (e.g., relocation, lifestyle change, etc.)?

- Identify a group of people in your city that is suffering and far from God. What creative step can you take to cross the religious, racial and socioeconomic boundaries to reach them with God's love (e.g., organize a team and study the needs of the group, create an alliance to help relieve the group's suffering)?

A prayer . . .

Jesus,

Reveal to me the group of people you want me to help. Show me the steps I need to take to relieve their suffering. Help me to connect with others who want to join me on this assignment.

AJITH FERNANDO'S MAJOR LIFE EVENTS

1963	Conversion to Christ
1972-1976	Studies at Asbury Seminary and Fuller Seminary
1976	Named national director of Sri Lanka Youth for Christ with a staff of ten
1983	Publishes first of fifteen books
1987	Speaks at first of four Urbana Missions Conferences
1995-2005	Youth for Christ establishes ministry centers throughout Sri Lanka
2010	Speaks to 4,300 leaders from 203 nations at Lausanne Congress in Cape Town
2011	Finishes 35 years as national director of Youth for Christ, Sri Lanka, with a staff of 152; appointed teaching director of Youth for Christ, Sri Lanka

Frances Hesselbein

SACRIFICE

*Leaving a Legacy Through Service
to Family, Community and Country*

LEARN: To serve is to live.

SUCCEED: Open doors for emerging leaders
and provide new opportunities.

Frances Hesselbein works in donated space across the street from
the magnificent St. Bartholomew's Episcopal Church on Park
Avenue in Manhattan. Visiting her office is like walking through
the life of one of America's most iconic leaders. Shelves are filled
with the books she and her peers have written. The awards she
has received, including twenty honorary doctoral degrees,[1] are too
numerous to display in her modest office.

Hesselbein has become a friend, mentor and hero. For someone
who travels frequently, she remains amazingly accessible. She has
spoken in sixty-eight countries, including England, Greece,

Kenya, South Africa, Iran, the Philippines, South Korea, China, Australia and New Zealand.[2]

I interviewed her on May 31, 2011, in the office of Leader to Leader Institute, now the Frances Hesselbein Leadership Institute. When our interview wound down, she gave me twenty-five articles to read. One of them, "3 Leadership Lessons," from a blog by Debbe Kennedy, mentioned three leadership characteristics that the author learned from Hesselbein.[3] After reading the entry, I filled in my own experiences that confirmed Kennedy's observations of Hesselbein's leadership qualities.

Unpretentious, warm and friendly. At an event in June 2011 with a small group of presidential council members for the New York City Leadership Center, Hesselbein arrived early. Jim Runyan, my board chairman, and I had several unhurried moments with her. She engaged with both of us personally, asking questions and offering encouragement with such comments as, "Your work inspires me and provides hope to New York City and its children." Then we watched as other members arrived. She was totally engaging, speaking to each one, expressing genuine interest. By the end of the meeting, every person agreed that her participation was the highlight.

That afternoon Hesselbein spent more time with us. Even though she had been traveling extensively, she made herself available. She stayed for dinner and joined us for a date at the opera.

Hesselbein understands and models the value of friendship among leadership. Leaders who interact with her all have the same reaction: "She is the kind of leader I want to become."

Values every person. Hesselbein makes each person with whom she interacts feel like the only person in the room. If you are having a conversation with her, she looks you in the eye and concentrates on what you are saying. Time after time I have seen her do this no matter who the person is. When I visit her office I feel as if I'm the only appointment on her agenda for the day.

Accessible and ready to help. I met Hesselbein four years ago through a mutual friend, John Clause of World Vision. I knew her schedule was full, so I thought this would be my only opportunity to ask her to join the National Advisory Team of our embryonic organization. She listened with great interest as I explained our goals and vision. Then she told me she would consider the invitation and respond in a week or two. Later that day she contacted a mutual friend and mentor, Bob Buford, who endorsed the idea. She called me the same day saying she would be honored to be a part of the team.

As a member of our team, she has put a warm and friendly face on our organization by speaking on our behalf more than a half dozen times. Her spirit of generosity, her genuine interest in other people and her joy in helping others achieve their goals has made her leadership style legendary.

DEFINING MOMENTS

Hesselbein entered college with dreams of writing poetry and drama. But at age seventeen, six weeks into her freshman year at the University of Pittsburgh's junior college in Johnstown, Pennsylvania, she was called home to her father's bedside. He was dying from complications of malaria contracted while serving in Panama and the Philippines. As he lay on his deathbed, Hesselbein looked into his eyes and promised him that she would take care of the family. "A tear rolled down my father's cheek. I kissed it and he was gone," she recalls.[4]

Her aunt and uncle invited her to live with them and attend Swarthmore College near Philadelphia. Although it seemed to be the sensible thing to do, going to Swarthmore would disrupt her family even more at a time when everyone was already fragile. Hesselbein made a decision based on what she believed was right even though it required personal sacrifice. She decided to stay home and fulfill her commitment to her father. This decision was an early indication of her unselfishness, and it became a determining factor in the direction of her future.

Hesselbein was not the first family member to sacrifice her own goals for the good of others. Her life of faith, service and sacrifice was shaped by ancestors who were lay preachers, soldiers, horseback-riding missionaries and historical preservationists.[5] Just as generations before her had answered the call to serve their country, she served her family. For five years after her father's death she worked and attended college classes at night and on weekends.[6]

At age twenty-two, Hesselbein married her husband, John. Shortly before he enlisted in the Navy during World War II, she gave birth to their son, John. Separated by thousands of miles, she decided to leave Pennsylvania and take their baby to join her husband, much to the dismay of her mother. Mama Wicks, her grandmother, settled it by saying, "Your place is with your husband." So Frances and baby John boarded the train and headed for Pensacola, and the next year moved from Pensacola to San Diego, to be with John.[7] Once again, Hesselbein sacrificed her own needs for those of her family.

Hesselbein's career with the Girl Scouts began when she became the leader of Troop 17 in her hometown. She had been asked multiple times to become a Girl Scout leader. This time she was being asked to take over for a leader who had left to become a missionary in India. Hesselbein had declined every request, saying that she was the mother of a little boy and knew nothing about leading young girls.

However, when she learned that thirty ten-year-old Girl Scouts meeting in the basement of the Second Presbyterian Church would be disbanded, she agreed to help for six weeks while they looked for a permanent leader.

Prior to her first meeting with the girls, Hesselbein studied the history of the Girl Scouts and learned that the organization had been founded eight years before women gained the right to vote in the United States. She was drawn to the organization because of its mission of helping "each girl reach her own highest potential," Hesselbein said. The global scope of the organization also appealed to Hesselbein, who had never traveled outside of the United States.

Hesselbein later realized that the principles of the Girl Scouts formed her leadership style. "They taught me the importance of hope and confidence," she said. "The self-confidence of my troop members was the strongest evidence of the priceless value of our shared experience."[8]

Hesselbein rose quickly through the ranks of leadership in the Girl Scouts organization. She served on the national board of directors and was appointed as one of six representatives to the Triennial World Conference in Greece.

"You could see the Parthenon from our meeting place," Hesselbein recalls, commenting on her first trip overseas. "It was the most amazing experience. . . . I met three hundred women from all over the world—Africa, Asia, Europe, Latin America and every continent—and everyone lived the Girl Scout Promise and the Law, sharing a common history tracing back to the original organization founded in 1912."[9]

She accepted her first Girl Scout professional position in Johnstown, Pennsylvania, serving for four years as CEO. She then became CEO of the Penn Lauren council in eastern Pennsylvania for two years. While there Hesselbein delivered a speech to her executive colleagues titled "What It Means to Belong." The speech described the power and influence of Girl Scouting to thwart societal forces keeping girls from growing up healthy.

As it turned out, the speech was timely. The Girl Scout organization was in search of a new national executive director, CEO, and her speech got the attention of the national office. Hesselbein was invited to New York City as a candidate for the position. She agreed to the interview at her husband's insistence. However, knowing that the organization had never in its sixty-four-year history hired from within,[10] she did not consider herself a serious candidate.

The Girl Scouts were going through a period of uncertainty; they had experienced eight consecutive years of decline. Knowing this, Hesselbein cast a vision for a new Girl Scouts. She believed a fresh organization could emerge that would be committed to its historic values and mission and yet be innovative. She described the Girl Scouts as "One Great Movement" of young girls effecting a quiet revolution—a revolution led by young women who were ethnically and racially representative of the broader culture. She recommended that the organization be restructured—from a traditional, hierarchical model to a circular model in which all 355 local councils would feel connected to the national office.

Hesselbein felt positive about the interview but skeptical that she would be seriously considered. However, to her surprise, she was offered the position. She accepted the offer and arrived in New York City on July 4, 1976, the nation's bicentennial. She describes the experience: "John and I watched the Tall Ships sail up the East River in celebration of the bicentennial from an apartment six blocks from Girl Scout headquarters at 830 Third Avenue. I had . . . left a small town in the mountains of western Pennsylvania to lead the largest organization for girls and women in the world."[11]

THE CONTEXT OF LEADERSHIP

Just as Hesselbein challenged the Girl Scouts in the 1970s and 1980s, she does the same for others today. Regarding public education in our country, she says "The house is on fire. Something must change or we cannot sustain the democracy." [12] And, regarding the situation of children in America, she has commented in numerous settings:

We have as many as 500,000 children today in New York City who will not graduate from high school. Across the nation we have an overall dropout rate of 30 percent . . . and 70 percent of children living in poverty will not graduate high school. Where there is no high school diploma, there is no hope.

Hesselbein sees the alarming relationship between high school dropouts and incarceration. When addressing the subject, she quotes Peter Drucker: "We live in a society that pretends to care about its children but it does not."[13]

When serving as "principal for a day" at the New School for Arts and Sciences, an alternative high school for at-risk young people in the South Bronx, New York, she asked the students, "If resources could be found, what are your school's greatest needs?" Their response: a library and textbooks—they had no textbooks. Hesselbein alerted her friends of the need, and they donated nineteen thousand dollars. With the contribution, the school created a library, and a call to the mayor's and chancellor's offices provided textbooks for all students. The school was adopted by Pfizer and Verizon. The next year, in a high school that had never had one college graduate, out of fifty-two graduates, nine members of the student council had college scholarships and one joined the Air Force.[14]

Although Hesselbein's sense of urgency is as great as ever, she also has great hope. As she travels to college campuses she sees a high level of interest in volunteering. Warren Bennis calls young people today "the crucible generation," and Hesselbein senses their hunger to make a difference.[15] She believes that they will rise up to become the next "greatest generation," a phrase popularized by Tom Brokaw.

CONSEQUENTIAL IMPACT

Management expert Peter Drucker was well acquainted with the world's most acclaimed CEOs—from GE's Jack Welch to Procter & Gamble's A. G. Lafley. Yet when asked by a journalist who he thought was the greatest leader in the country, Drucker instantly replied: Frances Hesselbein, the CEO of the American Girl Scout movement from 1976-1990.[16] Hesselbein also was named by *Fortune Magazine* as the "Best Nonprofit Manager in America."[17]

Jim Collins, who interviewed Hesselbein at the Living Leadership Conference in Atlanta on October 20, 2004, summarized her impact as a Level 5 leader who combines humility and will—someone who is fiercely ambitious for her organization but not for herself.

Under her leadership, membership grew to 2.25 million girls [after an eight-year decline], and a workforce mainly of volunteers that was 780,000 when she left [a 20 percent increase in thirteen years]. She received the Presidential Medal of Freedom in 1998, our nation's highest civilian honor.

But the signature of a Level 5 is what happens after you leave. Anyone who leaves an organization that declines is not Level 5. What happened? The great leader left, and the Girls Scouts grew to four million members. The great leader left, nearly one million volunteers. And now she's the chief leader of the Leader to Leader Institute [now The Frances Hesselbein Leadership Institute], whose very mission is the development of Level 5 in our society . . . creating leaders in all sectors.[18]

When presenting the Presidential Medal of Freedom to her, President Bill Clinton said this of Hesselbein: "She has shared her remarkable recipe for inclusion and excellence with countless organizations whose bottom line is measured not in dollars, but in changed lives. Among the noted hallmarks of her leadership style are openness to innovation, a willingness to share responsibility, and a respect for diversity."[19]

Inclusion. When Hesselbein came to New York City as the CEO of the Girl Scouts, only 5 percent of the girls in the movement were nonwhite. This was unacceptable to Hesselbein. She approached Vernon Jordan, president of the National Urban League, and requested that he ask Dr. Robert Hill, the researcher who had published *The Strengths of Black Families,* to do research for the Girl Scouts. She committed to pay whatever it would cost.[20] Vernon Jordan gave her Dr. Hill as his contribution.

Hill's breakthrough research taught the Girl Scouts how to connect with black, Hispanic and Native American young girls. They learned the expectations that each group had for its daughters. Hesselbein went to work on creating a new, inclusive image for the Girl Scouts, as she stated in an interview.

1. To the black community, the Girl Scouts communicated its history of helping one another. This addressed the intergenerational and community values of blacks in America.

2. To the Hispanic community, the Girl Scouts communicated that their daughters would be treasured and valued.

3. To Native Americans, the Girl Scouts communicated the value of being "the original people." Using the phrase, "Your names are on the rivers," the Girl Scouts told Native Americans that their identity was recognized and appreciated.

The Girl Scouts changed their logo to reflect the value of every culture and redesigned materials to emphasize inclusion. The change went beyond a marketing campaign, however. It reached deep into programming. Hesselbein wanted to enhance the opportunity for girls to compete in an increasingly technological age,[21] so she had scholars guide a major curriculum revision. Under her leadership, new Girl Scout handbooks focused on math, science and technology.

During Hesselbein's thirteen years at the head of Girl Scouts, the membership of minority girls and women tripled. This contributed to the growth of the Girl Scouts into a richly diverse, cohesive, inclusive organization.

Innovation. Inclusion was one factor in the revitalization of the Girl Scouts, and innovation was another. Hesselbein and her team abandoned the traditional, hierarchical structure and introduced a model of "circular management." With 355 councils spread across the nation, a culture where everyone was respected and heard was essential. Listening skills became a necessity at every level of the organization. "When we open up the organization, dispersing the leadership, including people from across the enterprise," says Hesselbein, "there is a new energy, a new synergy." Within five years the Girls Scouts totally transformed the organization.[22]

One of the first things Hesselbein did as CEO of the Girl Scouts was to recruit John Creedon, the new CEO of MetLife. He helped her raise ten million dollars to build the Edith Macy Conference Center, a training center. In 1989, more than two thousand adult volunteers were trained in top-level seminars on service, marketing, financial planning, property management and other topics. Tens of thousands of others, from volunteer troop leaders to the executive directors of councils, went through local training programs.[23]

Honoring our military institutions. Family history and military involvement are the fabric of Hesselbein's life. On Memorial Day, the day prior to our interview, Hesselbein made sure that flowers were planted on family grave sites, which she has been doing for decades as an act of remembrance for generations of soldiers.[24]

In 2009, she was invited to serve as the class of '51 chair for the study of leadership at West Point. "I have come with an empty notebook," she told the five colonels and the major, the team who would work with her. "I cannot have a plan until I know your expectations." Part of her legacy is helping everyone—from military elites to entry-level clerks—believe that they are leaders.[25]

After two years in her position on the faculty at West Point, she said this in her farewell speech: "My son, my father, my brother, my husband—and our ancestors—back through history. . . . From the American Revolution on, from our family's soldiers, I learned, 'When called, we serve. To serve is to live.'"[26]

Hesselbein's autobiographical book on leadership captures her core philosophy and practice. I summarized five of her most important leadership axioms, which she also spoke about in our interview.

We manage for the mission, we manage for innovation and we manage for diversity.[27] Hesselbein speaks forcefully on the topic of focus. She was invited by President Reagan to come to Washington,

D. C., to consider a Cabinet-level position with his administration. She considered the invitation the greatest honor in her life, but she declined. At the time, the Girl Scouts were in a major transition, and her role there gave her a better opportunity to fulfill her personal mission: to help each girl reach her own highest potential. She never uses the word *problem*. Where others see problems, she sees opportunities for innovation. Inclusion is her highest operating value, and it speaks volumes in a nation where people of different cultures are often the most disadvantaged.

Be ye an opener of doors (Emerson).[28] Hesselbein's leadership philosophy is rooted in creating opportunity for others, especially those less fortunate. Her heart breaks over the multitude of young people without a high school education and with little hope for the future. She treasures her involvement in the Bright China Social Fund, which builds hundreds of schools in China's poorest villages.[29]

The first item in your budget should be learning, education and the development of your people. Hesselbein partnered with John Creedon to raise the funds to build the Edith Macy Conference Center on four hundred wooded acres in Westchester County, forty-five minutes from New York City. The state-of-the-art facilities helped the leadership teams, volunteers and staff in the Girl Scouts to see themselves as being essential in leading "One Great Movement."[30]

Do your research before you effect change.[31] Hesselbein's three-month research project on diversity and inclusion paved the way for more than a million additional girls and volunteers to join the Girl Scouts. In the words of Peter Drucker, Hesselbein was able to "look out the window" and see the changes that needed to be made. Solid research informed her choices.

Find the best minds in whatever field and take them as mentors.[32] Hesselbein became a devotee of Peter Drucker long before meeting him. She devoured his writings on management. Eventually they met, and Drucker became her long-term mentor and coach—the father of modern management mentored the woman who led the world's largest organization for women. Hesselbein left the Girl Scouts after thirteen years and founded the Leader to Leader Institute (originally the Peter Drucker Foundation). And she keeps the legacy of Drucker alive through award-winning publications produced every year by Leader to Leader—now the Frances Hesselbein Leadership Institute.

VISION

As Hesselbein looks across the landscape of our nation, her greatest concern is the increase in school dropout rates and incarceration of young people. Her greatest hope is to see communities of faith adopt a public school, and she challenges churches and civic-minded groups to do so. Some public schools have no textbooks. Other schools need mentors to help underperforming students. She believes that public schools are the "soul of the city," the place where children can find opportunity, and that from the beginning of our country, there have been two institutions that have sustained the democracy—the U.S. Army and public education.

She sees three signs of hope in public education: first, the charter school movement; second, individual initiatives to help inner-city schools; third, a growing movement of volunteerism in our public schools. However, the need is so great that Hesselbein believes it will take a revolution of like-minded citizens to continue to help the public schools to sustain our democracy.

LEADER APPLICATION

- Ask God to help you identify a group in need that he wants you to serve long term (e.g., children, homeless, fatherless).
- Thank God for those who have gone before and sacrificed to make your life possible (e.g., parents, soldiers, educators).

A prayer . . .

Jesus,

Our hearts swell with gratitude for those who have gone on before us. May we live our lives in an exemplary way for those who will follow us.

FRANCES HESSELBEIN'S MAJOR LIFE EVENTS

1976	Named national executive director, CEO, of Girl Scouts USA
1980	Peter Drucker declares the Girl Scouts the best-managed organization in the country
1990	Leaves the Girl Scouts and founds the Leader to Leader Institute
1998	Receives from President Clinton the U.S. Presidential Medal of Freedom, our country's highest civilian honor
2009	University of Pittsburgh creates the Hesselbein Global Academy for Student Leadership and Civic Engagement; appointed as the class of '51 chair for the study of leadership at West Point Military Academy
2011	Publishes autobiography, *My Life in Leadership*
2012	Leader to Leader Institute Board changes name to the Frances Hesselbein Leadership Institute

W. Wilson Goode Sr.

EQUALITY

The Courage to Effect Change

LEARN: Understand the grim reality of imprisonment in America and its consequences. Discover that one courageous leader can achieve greater results than anyone predicts.

SUCCEED: Have a vision that is informed by faith. Be determined. Work hard. Be available. Demonstrate humility.

Wilson Goode carries himself with a regal presence, but his true dignity comes from within, as I have learned since meeting him in 1998.

We became acquainted at Eastern Baptist Theological Seminary (now Palmer Seminary). He had finished his second term as mayor of Philadelphia in 1992 and was working in the United States Department of Education. Both of us were incoming students in the

Doctorate of Ministry program, the Renewal of the Church for Mission. We had signed on to study under Ray Bakke.

I wondered why someone approaching his sixtieth birthday, who had achieved so much already, would start this degree with a group of unknown ministry leaders, many from modest-size churches. Over the next three years I learned why Goode chose to be in the program—he is a voracious, lifelong learner. When the class did its intensive in New York City, Goode's eyes lit up to see church after church radically changing their neighborhoods.

Our visit to Bethel Gospel Assembly in Harlem inspired Goode's doctoral thesis: "From Clubhouse to Lighthouse." He studied churches like Bethel that reached inner-city youth through basketball programs, housed homeless men in a discipleship program and had a robust global missions program.

When I asked Goode what the New York City course had meant to him, he said, "The immersion was remarkable. I saw fresh models and passionate leaders who are changing one neighborhood at a time."

In his own community, however, Goode saw congregants commuting into blighted urban neighborhoods for Sunday service without seriously investing themselves in the transformation of that neighborhood. Goode is a doer, and he was determined to change the culture of congregations.

For our June 2000 graduation, Goode hosted our entire class and their families at his home for a dinner. He arranged a horse-drawn carriage tour of Philadelphia for my family. We will never forget that experience.

In the nearly fifteen years that we have known one another, I have often asked Goode to come and speak in New York City. He has said yes every time. His credibility in African American circles is largely unmatched. He is one of the most accessible, gracious and kind leaders I have ever met. In 2007, he joined the National Advisory Team of the New York City Leadership Center.

DEFINING MOMENTS

Born in 1938, Goode was the sixth of seven children born to an illiterate North Carolina sharecropper. Goode was introduced early to the injustice of the then-common practice of sharecropping. "We only received 20 percent of the proceeds," he said, "barely enough to survive. And we moved every year from one farm to the next."[1]

A photo[2] of his tiny wood-frame birthplace, taken in 1983 after Goode won the Democratic primary in Philadelphia's mayoral race, symbolizes the powerful contrast between his past and his future—from the grinding poverty of sharecropping to the pinnacle of political influence in America's fourth-largest city.

Goode's values were learned from his mother. When a white hobo came to their front door asking for food, Goode's mother graciously fed him until he was full. Moved by his mother's generosity, Goode ran after the man when he left. "Mr. Hobo, Mr. Hobo," he called. When he finally caught up with him, Goode handed him five dollars, the entire amount of his savings for the past five years.

Although the hobo had the same racial background as the landowners who took advantage of his family in the sharecropping system, Goode saw the humanity in him that transcended race. "It was my first opportunity to extend generosity to someone even less fortunate than myself," said Goode.[3] Like his mother, Goode was baptized in the Jordan River near their home. His identity was deeply shaped by her spirituality.

His father taught him important lessons as well. He learned the value of fairness and equality, that nothing happens without hard work, and that you get out of life exactly what you put into it. Goode had a conflicted relationship with his father, however. "My father was a perfect role model six days a week," says Goode. "Yet every Friday when he got paid he drank and became violent." When Goode was fourteen, his father was sent to jail for three years for physically hurting Goode's mom and their landlord.[4]

Decades later, Goode reflected on this time of separation from his father. In a sermon, he said, "Jesus' greatest agony was not His crucifixion, but His separation from His Father."[5] For Goode, the separation from his father helped him identify with the fatherless children of prison inmates. This holy discontent fueled Goode's motivation for the next sixty years as he mobilized one of the most significant mentoring initiatives in American history with the Amachi program.

About the time his father went to prison, his family moved to Philadelphia, where they shared a home with two other families. Goode had counted on Philadelphia being the "promised land," but the home they lived in there was worse than the one they left in North Carolina. "There was no space, no yard and no privacy," said Goode. It was two years before the family had their own home.[6]

As Goode prepared to graduate high school, he wondered what to do next. His guidance counselor told him to not even consider going to college. But another voice was giving him different advice. Rev. William Lemon and his wife, Muriel Providence, insisted that he do exactly that. They saw great potential in the stuttering country boy from North Carolina, and they became his heroes for life.[7]

Public service. Goode finished college, joined the military to complete his ROTC requirements, sold insurance and married Velma, his high school sweetheart. They later had three children: Muriel, Wilson Jr. and Natasha. In 1966, Goode landed a job in public service. Over the next twelve years, his responsibilities rapidly expanded.

As the president for the Philadelphia Council for Community Advancement, Goode and his team created two thousand jobs in eight years working with fifty groups. Goode was emerging as a skillful administrator. Having experienced substandard housing firsthand, he had a passion for serving the underserved of his city.

At the invitation of Governor Milton Shapp, Goode became the first African American to serve as the commissioner of the Pennsylvania Public Utility and very quickly became chairman of the commission. Goode managed a few dozen employees, and his effectiveness in this post led to his rapid advancement back in Philadelphia.

Goode was asked to become managing director of Philadelphia, giving oversight to thirty thousand employees. In 1972, the Junior Chamber of Commerce in Philadelphia named Goode Young Leader of the Year when he was thirty-five. By this time, Goode had become one of the most high-profile African American leaders in Philadelphia, and he was an enormous source of pride for his community. Goode's goal was simple: to bring the greatest amount of equality to the greatest number of people in Philadelphia.

When I asked Goode what he had learned from his rapid advancement in public service, he was quick to answer: "When opportunity knocks, be prepared to answer. If you take the leap, additional opportunities will happen. And pay attention to detail and understand the goal before you."

In 1982, when Goode was managing director under Mayor Bill Green, there were strong racial tensions between the Philadelphia police and the African American community. African American leaders urged Goode to run for mayor and become the first African American mayoral candidate in Philadelphia's two-hundred-year history. A "Draft Goode" movement rapidly gained momentum.

Goode was conflicted. He had been appointed by Mayor Green, and he expected Green to run for reelection. He was torn between his loyalty to Green and the appeal of his community. To the tremendous disappointment of his community, Goode decided to wait four years before running.

But in a surprise announcement in November 1982, Green announced that he would not be running for reelection. So in December, Goode declared his candidacy. Goode had no strategy or structure—just a deep sense of divine timing. He would be running for mayor in a city that had lost 150,000 jobs in fifteen years.[8]

In his campaign, Goode received the greatest amount of support from the black churches. The Black Clergy of Philadelphia and the Baptist Minister's Conference represented 400,000 black Philadelphians. "Members of congregations knew I was no pseudo-religious Christian coming to church to capture a few votes," Goode said in his autobiography. "My candidacy for mayor was not an indication of the greatness of Wilson Goode but a witness to the power of God."[9]

Goode went on to defeat Frank Rizzo, a political legend in Philadelphia, in the Democratic primary. Thousands of black people helped register more than 100,000 other black people to elect a black man as the first African American mayor of their city. African American voters turned out for the election in record numbers—for the first time in more than two hundred years, someone who looked like them could be their mayor.

Goode won the general election by 123,000 votes. He describes the moment when the results were announced and his family entered Convention Hall.

> I was moved beyond belief as I felt a wellspring of emotions flood my soul and rise up in my throat. It was one of the most emotional moments of my life. Without thinking, this reserved, low-key public servant walked on the platform, threw his fist in the air, and leaped for joy! It was the most incredible moment of my life.[10]

Two hundred and eight years after declaring to the world that "we hold these truths to be self-evident, that all men are created equal," the city that gave the country its vision for independence elected its first African American mayor. Wilson Goode challenged the citizens of Philadelphia to join him when he asked, "I want to build a better Philadelphia—will you help me?"

A new career at sixty. About the time Goode was graduating from his doctoral program, John DiIulio, President Bush's director for the White House faith-based initiative, invited Goode to help with Amachi, a faith-based mentoring initiative for children of incarcerated parents.

He expected Goode to "lend a hand, pass along a name, possibly contribute a few consulting hours, and perhaps give a speech. DiIulio was astonished when Goode did virtually all the initial legwork himself."[11] Goode explained to me that he recruited the first four hundred volunteers himself. He was passionate about this cause because it was rooted so deeply in his own boyhood journey from North Carolina.[12]

But where would the children come from? Goode went to correctional facilities in Philadelphia and asked mothers if they would like someone to mentor their children while they were in prison. Referring to Goode's involvement with Amachi, Amy Rosenberg wrote, "It is a beautiful mission—in its simplicity and in the way it dovetails with the painful episodes of Goode's life."[13]

Goode is always eager to tell the story of Amachi. He begins by explaining that the word *Amachi* is a West African word that means "who knows but what God has brought us through this child." The model is simple—one mentor for one child for one hour per week for one year. It is also profoundly successful. In 2003 the U.S. Health and Human Services Department adopted it as a model and now awards funds to churches and organizations that replicate its mentoring.

"I grieve about incarceration every day," Goode says. "America incarcerates more people than any other country in the world. The goal is to dismantle, piece by piece, the prison industrial complex in America, one child at a time."[14]

According to one study in eighteen states with large prison populations, a majority of inmates are black. In Ohio, where the black population is 12 percent, the black prison population is 52 percent. In Illinois, the black population is 15 percent, and the black prison population is 65 percent. States with the largest percentage of black inmates are outlined in table 9.1.

Table 9.1. Percentage of Inmates Who Are Black.

Alabama (65)	Louisiana (76)	North Carolina (64)
Arkansas (52)	Maryland (77)	Ohio (52)
California (69)	Michigan (55)	Pennsylvania (56)
Delaware (63)	Mississippi (75)	South Carolina (69)
Georgia (64)	New Jersey (64)	Tennessee (53)
Illinois (65)	New York (51)	Virginia (68)

In every state, the percentage of inmates who are black is at least double the percentage of the overall black population. But in Pennsylvania, where Goode started Amachi, the percentage was almost six times greater (10 percent of the general population was black; 56 percent of the prison population was black). Those who are black are seven times more likely to be imprisoned than those who are white.[15]

Michelle Alexander calls this "The New Jim Crow," which is the title of her book. In a Huffington Post article by the same title, she states:

- There are more African Americans under correctional control today—in prison or jail, on probation or parole—than were enslaved in 1850, a decade before the Civil War began.

- As of 2004, more African American men were disenfranchised (due to felon disenfranchisement laws) than in 1870.

- A large majority of African American men in some urban areas, like Chicago, have been labeled felons for life. These men are part of a growing undercaste—not class, *caste*—a group of people who are permanently relegated, by law, to an inferior second-class status.[16]

The United States has the highest rate of imprisonment in the world. More than seven million people are under correctional supervision.[17] Although we have only 5 percent of the global population, we have nearly 25 percent of the global prison population.[18] Nationally, 60 percent of our prison population is made up of blacks and Hispanics.

CONSEQUENTIAL IMPACT

During his eight years as mayor of Philadelphia, Goode achieved some remarkable milestones. Prior to his coming into office, no downtown buildings were allowed to be higher than the "top of William Penn's hat," referring to the downtown statue of one of the city's most celebrated citizens. Goode changed that and remade the Philadelphia skyline. Gleaming skyscrapers now attract businesses and jobs to the city.

Goode launched a Center City revival with the Convention Center, the Center City District, the Anti-Graffiti Network, the internationally renowned Mural Arts Program and initiatives to help the homeless. He opened up opportunities to minorities and women in city departments, boards and top city positions, including police commissioner.[19]

Current mayor of Philadelphia Michael Nutter said, "The triumph of Goode's 1983 election was singular. It created a coalition that continues to influence city politics. Of the major cities that elected their first African American mayors in the '80s . . . Philadelphia is the only one to have elected a second and a third."[20]

In slightly more than a decade, Goode's leadership in Amachi has netted 300,000 mentors for children of incarcerated parents in fifty states. More than one thousand agencies are involved in implementing Amachi. In a moving video, Goode describes the moment he met a grandfather, a father and a son.

I went to a prison and saw a grandfather, a father, and a grandson, all in the same prison at the same time, and they told me that they met for the first time in prison. When I was about to leave, the grandson pulled me aside and told me that he too had a son who he had not seen, and he presumed he would meet him for the first time in prison also. . . . It is possible to have four generations in prison at the same time.[21]

The Amachi program influenced President George W. Bush to appeal for volunteers nationally in 2001. In 2003, the president was successful in convincing Congress to give fifty million dollars in funding to mobilize mentors for children of prisoners.

By 2003, Amachi, in partnership with Big Brothers Big Sisters, had established ten locations outside Philadelphia. The Amachi Training Institute had been set up in 2002. More than 3,500 people have been trained in the process of establishing Amachi programs.[22] More recently, Goode's team received a $17.8 million federal grant from the Office of Juvenile Justice and Delinquency Prevention to spread the Amachi programs to thirty-eight states.

Now in his seventies, Goode continues to work tirelessly on behalf of these children. He is fueled by the conviction that without a mentor, the child of a prisoner has a 70 percent probability of becoming a prisoner.[23]

Goode's enduring impact continues to be felt by his family and church community. His son, Wilson Jr., has followed his father's footsteps into politics and has been a member of the Philadelphia City Council for twelve years. Goode preaches forty times a year in churches across the country and serves as the pastor of administration at First Baptist Church of Paschal,[24] which has been his home church for many years. Commenting on his fifty-seven-year marriage to his wife, Velma, Goode said, "If she ever left me, I told her I am going with her."[25]

WHAT IS YOUR VISION FOR A JUST SOCIETY?

I want to see pastors and professionals providing bold and prophetic leadership. We need an alliance of clergy, marketplace leaders and politicians working together to reduce the prison population by half in the next generation.

VISION

Looking over the landscape of our rapidly growing prison population and the decimation of communities of color, Goode states the following priorities:

We need to make every effort to enlarge early childhood learning programs and create learning centers where the private sector gives philanthropically to assist the community's preschool children through early education programs.

We need the rapid expansion of charter schools or top-notch grade schools so that every child can read by the third grade. Future prison populations are forecast on the basis of third-grade reading levels.

All 1.5 million children of prisoners need a mentor. Faith-based groups are in the best position to mature a movement of mentoring that could change the trajectory of an entire generation.

We need strong reentry programs for prisoners. Just as Goode's father returned to the family and his parents celebrated fifty years of marriage, all prisoners can be returned to society with the opportunity for a productive life.

We need to roll back the severe sentencing guidelines. In the United States, two thousand juveniles are currently sentenced to life imprisonment compared to very few in the rest of the world combined. Ten-year sentences for certain crimes are unjust punishment. A child loses a parent for his or her entire childhood when prison sentences do not fit the offense.[26]

Goode envisions a day when every school system has an early childhood development program. He believes that 90 percent of the U.S. population can reach the ninth grade or higher. He is praying that God will convince every elected official that a competitive education is the number one strategy to improve the welfare of every American. "There is an urgent need to create educational systems with productive teachers who are held accountable with performance pay," he says. "Unproductive teachers need to be let go."

Looking at the 2011 "Arab Spring" in the Middle East, Goode sees a warning sign about what happens when young people have insufficient opportunities. Eventually they rise up and challenge the government through protest and riots. "Young people refuse to be sentenced to a future that they have no part in," says Goode.[27]

LEADER APPLICATION

- Have you ever visited a prison in your community? If not, consider joining a local outreach ministry to those who are incarcerated.

- Participate in or support a local effort to mentor children of incarcerated parents.

- Use your influence to start an alliance of clergy, marketplace leaders and politicians who will work together to improve education and reduce the prison population.

  A prayer . . .

Jesus,

Help your people draft and support legislation that will create a more just system for those who are needlessly incarcerated. Show us how we can be your presence to those in prison and their children.

WILSON GOODE SR.'S MAJOR LIFE EVENTS

1938	Born to sharecropper family in Seaboard, North Carolina
1954	Moves to Philadelphia
1968	Director, Philadelphia Council for Community Advancement
1978	Chairman of Pennsylvania Utilities Commission
1980	Managing director, City of Pennsylvania
1984	Mayor of Philadelphia
1992	Deputy assistant secretary, U.S. Department of Education
2000	Receives doctoral degree from Eastern Baptist Theological Seminary
	Organizes Amachi/Public Private Venture
2006	Recipient of the Purpose Prize for Amachi Leadership

George Gallup Jr.

BELONGING

The Power of Knowledge and the Importance of Faith

LEARN: Belonging comes before believing. Good research
serves as a "siren" to society.

SUCCEED: Use good research as the basis for important
personal and policy decisions.

George Gallup Jr. was just a few years short of celebrating his
eightieth birthday, yet he took the bus to Port Authority and
walked fifteen blocks to our 57th Street luncheon meeting. It was
a hot, steamy day in mid-July 2008, and Gallup came in soaking
wet but smiling. Despite the heat and the long walk, he was
buoyant. His eyes twinkled despite the perspiration.

Meeting George Gallup, whose family name is iconic in America,
was like being reacquainted with a long-lost friend. Although he
knew little about me, I felt as if I knew him well. The warmth of his
personality drew me in, and I connected with his childlike exu-

berance for life and faith. He spoke tenderly of his wife, Kingsley, who had died the year before. I had known him as a man of great influence, but I came to know him as a man of great kindness.

Since then I enjoyed meals with Gallup and stayed with him in his home. I saw the extension of his kindness to his community and beyond. His adopted dog, Lamar (named after Senator Lamar Alexander from Tennessee), was so attached that he never let Gallup out of his sight. He even jumped into the pool whenever Gallup went for a swim.

GEORGE GALLUP JR., 1930-2011

George Gallup Jr. passed away on November 21, 2011, in Princeton, New Jersey, the city that had been his lifelong home. His memorial service was held in the Princeton University Chapel. Gallup was one of the early graduates of the Princeton religion department. In one of our final phone calls in the fall of 2011, Gallup commented, "I am so thankful for the opportunity to be a part of the faith community. God really renewed my life deeply in the past twenty-five years."

DEFINING MOMENTS

To write about George Gallup Jr. without including a brief history of his famous family would paint an incomplete picture.

Gallup's father entered the world of polling, in part, to help his mother-in-law, Ola Babcock Miller (Gallup Jr.'s maternal grandmother), win election as Iowa's secretary of state in 1932. She won the election, becoming the first female to hold that office, and was reelected twice.

In 1935, Gallup Sr. started the Gallup organization. Taking seriously the core value of democracy, he was adamant about reporting the will of the people. He often stated his core mission in these words: "If democracy is supposed to be based on the will of the people, then somebody should go out and find out what that will is."[1] And that is what he did. Determined to maintain objectivity, he refused to accept research projects sponsored by special interest groups. This defining decision set the organization on a course that established its credibility and built its reputation for fairness and accuracy. As a result, the Gallup organization became the leading influence in the polling industry.[2]

The Gallup organization surveys as many as one thousand people a day, 350 days a year. The work of Gallup Sr. demonstrated that different cultures could work together to address the great global needs of the world.[3]

For some people, being born into a well-known, influential family is their downfall. But instead of trying to define himself by cutting himself off from his family roots, George Gallup Jr. built on his father's legacy and created his own identity. One of the unfinished projects of his life was writing the complete biography of his father's legacy in the polling industry.

Gallup had his first personal experience with God at age nine. "I remember hearing a male voice say, 'be good,'" he recalls. Soon after that a friend invited him to an Episcopalian church, which he started to attend. Although his father taught him a sense of God's loving care, his parents were not active in the church. The Episcopal church was the first place where Gallup had a sense of spiritual belonging. The church became his spiritual home, the place where he was welcomed and where his soul was nourished. At age ten, Gallup began to develop a sense of personal responsibility for his faith decisions.

In 1949, Gallup enrolled in Princeton University and became a religion major in one of the nation's first religion departments. The intellectual rigors of Princeton tested his faith, but the brilliant and clear thinking of such writers as Brother Lawrence (*The Practice of the Presence of God*), C. S. Lewis (*Mere Christianity*) and Dietrich Bonhoeffer (*The Cost of Discipleship*) helped him realize that faith could be rational; he did not need to turn off his mind to practice faith.

Gallup combined his interest in spiritual matters with his family's expertise in polling to study America's belief in God for his senior thesis. His research revealed that people fell into four categories of religious belief:

Authoritarian—following a rigid system of rules

Empirical—sensing God in nature; experiencing healing

Rational—relying on reason

Volitional—being practical (i.e., it's safer to believe than not to believe)

The biggest response was in the empirical faith category. A significant number of Americans based their faith on experience rather than on an intellectual understanding of truth. This information lodged in Gallup's mind and influenced his life's work. It set him on a course of using research as a way to help Christians understand that faith and reason are compatible; they are friends, not foes.

After college, Gallup became assistant rector at an Episcopal church in Galveston, Texas, where most of the members were Bahamian. Gallup's job was to teach the Bible and organize the baseball team. This was a time of spiritual formation for him, as he met people whose faith determined their daily lives and choices rather than vice versa. He felt a sense of belonging among them even though his skin color was different from theirs. He learned from them that true Christian community transcends ethnicity.[4]

For the next twenty years, Gallup concentrated on research for the Gallup organization, and his involvement with church waned. His three children grew up and moved on with their careers and family. In the book *Under God's Power,* Gallup describes this season of his faith journey as one of complacency. "I was relating to God on my own terms. Everything was going great, so I began to go through the motions in my faith."[5]

The death of both his parents in the early 1980s shook Gallup deeply. He sensed a need for a renewal of faith in himself as well as in the American church. He also experienced a series of health and family problems. Speaking of what he learned during this time, Gallup said, "Without suffering, one will not know God's grace. God will meet us if we come to Him."[6]

As he observed American churches, he saw few that were focusing on the uniqueness of Christ. In response to that observation, he began changing the direction of his research, increasingly focusing on the influence of religion around the world. A major global research project to survey religious belief, one of the largest undertaken, is now under way.

During this time Gallup was influenced by the writings of Henri Nouwen, the great Catholic contemplative thinker and writer. Nouwen's ideas, along with those of Peter Moore from Trinity School of Ministry, led Gallup and Kingsley into a season of renewal. As part of a small group, they recognized the power that is unleashed in people when they experience a sense of belonging and unity in Jesus Christ.

In 1986, Billy Graham invited Gallup to Amsterdam '86. Sponsored by the Billy Graham Evangelistic Association (BGEA), Amsterdam '86 brought together 8,000 traveling evangelists from approximately 180 nations for 10 days. It was touted as the largest gathering held solely for those on the front lines of the gospel.

In Amsterdam, Gallup became familiar with the guiding philosophy of the BGEA: to affirm its own core Christian beliefs and then to invite all who share those beliefs to join them in ministry. This cornerstone conviction allowed hundreds of diverse groups to become partners. For Gallup personally, this concept affirmed his conviction about the power and effectiveness of belonging, and it energized his renewal of faith. He emerged from that event as a spokesperson for the type of evangelical faith practiced by the BGEA.[7]

Because of his outspoken faith, his knowledge of culture, and his love for Christ and the church, Gallup often was called on to advise and represent other Christian agencies. Among them was Alpha, an organization birthed in London by the Anglican church Hampton Trinity Brompton (now known as HTB). Alpha focuses on the basic tenets of Christianity and affirms them in small group settings. Over a ten-week period, Alpha participants meet for meals and a presentation on various aspects of the Christian faith. Partway through the study, participants are invited to a "Holy Spirit Weekend" where many experience conversion to Christianity. The emphasis on small groups was particularly significant to Gallup because it addressed the need people have to belong to something meaningful.

CONSEQUENTIAL IMPACT

In 1984, Gallup published the book *Forecast 2000,* in which he identified nine "forces" that would shape America in the next twenty years. The number one force he identified was war and terrorism. The chapter opens with a fictional account of an event that is eerily similar to the dramatic, nonfictional events that unfolded seventeen years later on September 11, 2001. The fictional setting was 1997 in New York City on a warm spring afternoon. A terrorist group commandeered the observation deck of the Empire State Building and threatened to use a nuclear device. They chose New York City because it has the largest Jewish population of any city in the world.

Gallup's plot came from polling results that the Gallup agency had been collecting and interpreting. Gallup used this example to support his belief that research provides an important, early warning system for the culture.

Research today, he told me, indicates "that the majority of African Americans in Detroit do not have enough money to buy groceries—creating riot conditions. Additionally, we live in a culture of sexual chaos where the majority of young women have contracted a sexually transmitted disease by the age of twenty-five. These, he says, are important sirens in our culture."[8]

In 1988, four years after the death of Gallup Sr., the Gallup organization launched the Gallup International Institute, a not-for-profit foundation to research America's religious and spiritual values. The mission of the institute is to "discover, test and implement new ideas for the betterment of society."[9] One of its special focuses is youth. The institute has produced many widely read publications that have influenced the direction for youth ministry and education.

THE MOST WIDELY READ PUBLICATIONS OF THE GALLUP INTERNATIONAL INSTITUTE ARE:

1. *The Religious Life of Young Americans: A Compendium of Surveys on the Spiritual Beliefs and Practices of Teenagers and Young Adults*

2. *America's Youth in the 1990s*

3. *The Gallup Survey on Teenage Suicide*

4. *The Spiritual Life of Young Americans: Approaching the Year 2000*

5. *Teen Suicide: A Report on the 1991 Gallup Survey Among Teens and the 1994 Gallup Update Survey*

6. *The Bible and the American People*

7. *Teenage Attitudes and Behavior Concerning Tobacco: Report of the Findings*

8. *Youthviews*[10]

Much of Gallup's research has concentrated on American religious life. In his book *Surveying the Religious Landscape,* he notes gaps between the belief and behaviors of people who identify themselves as "born again." In regard to beliefs about reincarnation, fortune tellers and astrology, he found little difference between those who claimed to be born again and those who did not.[11] In regard to beliefs about the afterlife, he concluded that "people anticipate a great deal of spiritual angst. . . . People fear that they will not be loved by God, and expect to find an emptiness."[12]

Love of God: Beliefs, Practices and Characteristics

For each of the following statements, please tell me where you would place yourself on a scale from 0 to 5, if 0 stands for "does not apply at all" and 5 stands for "applies completely."

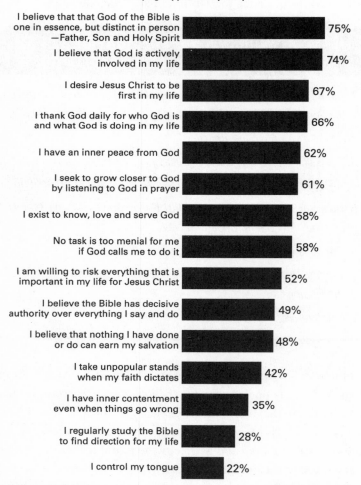

% saying "applies completely"

Statement	%
I believe that that God of the Bible is one in essence, but distinct in person—Father, Son and Holy Spirit	75%
I believe that God is actively involved in my life	74%
I desire Jesus Christ to be first in my life	67%
I thank God daily for who God is and what God is doing in my life	66%
I have an inner peace from God	62%
I seek to grow closer to God by listening to God in prayer	61%
I exist to know, love and serve God	58%
No task is too menial for me if God calls me to do it	58%
I am willing to risk everything that is important in my life for Jesus Christ	52%
I believe the Bible has decisive authority over everything I say and do	49%
I believe that nothing I have done or do can earn my salvation	48%
I take unpopular stands when my faith dictates	42%
I have inner contentment even when things go wrong	35%
I regularly study the Bible to find direction for my life	28%
I control my tongue	22%

Figure 10.1. *Source:* George H. Gallup Jr., "How Are American Christians Living Their Faith?" *gpns Commentary,* August 19, 2003 <www.gallup.com/poll/9088/how-american-christians-living-their-faith.aspx>.

A 2003 Gallup poll that collected data about religious beliefs and practices confirmed the contrast between what people say they believe and what difference that belief makes in the way they live. For example, the survey showed that 74 percent of respondents believe that God is actively involved in their lives. But only 28 percent study the Bible to find direction. And only 22 percent say they have control over their tongue. (See figure 10.1.)

According to Gallup's interpretation, this indicates that people still encounter God and faith "empirically" rather than from their confidence in the truth of Scripture. Their faith does not result in the strength to defend it, the courage to put it into practice or the conviction that it makes a difference.

WHAT IS YOUR UNDERSTANDING OF HOW PEOPLE RELATE TO THEIR FAITH?

Having reflected on my own spiritual renewal and the propensity of churchgoers to base their faith on experience rather than knowledge, I have concluded that close community relationships are more important than ever for maintaining robust intellectual faith. People need to belong before they believe; they need to believe before they will engage; and they need to engage before they will commit. I see small group ministry as the basis for a vibrant faith community. Increasing the number of engaged people in a church by merely 1 percent will translate into a significant increase in volunteerism and financial contributions.

Gallup had weekly small group meetings in his home for as long as his health allowed. He believed they are the antidote to the weakening family and the buttress against a hostile world. Healthy community is essential for the successful navigation of life's challenges, and small groups are the most effective way to communicate life-changing patterns of following Christ.

VISION

Gallup was convinced that research would continue to give insight into the biggest problems on the planet. Polls give people a voice in their destiny, and the results enable economies to become more efficient and churches to become more effective.

He believed that a revival of spiritual understanding would eventually bring a return to civility and a turning away from selfish values, and that a return to Judeo-Christian values would reverse America's self-destructive trajectory.

Gallup was convinced that a sense of belonging, achieved through Christ-centered small groups, is the key element of a national renewal. He looked forward to a time when a spiritual awakening, rooted in prayer, would bring about a revitalized sense of the presence of God.

LEADER APPLICATION

- What could be done in your home or local church to create a greater sense of belonging (e.g., expand the work of hospitality, begin small group communities)?

- Consider doing a survey of your church or community to determine the greatest needs (physical, spiritual, social). Develop a plan to act on the results.

  A prayer . . .

Jesus,

Awaken me to the needs of my community through careful conversations. Help me to be creative in responding to those needs in concert with my family of faith.

GEORGE GALLUP JR.'S MAJOR LIFE EVENTS

1932	Gallup Sr. uses research to assist mother-in-law to become secretary of state in Iowa
1935	Gallup Organization is founded
1940	Gallup Jr. begins to attend church as a nine-year-old
1949	Enters Princeton University's religion department
1960-1980	Builds research practice
1984	Writes *Forecast 2000*
1986	Attends Amsterdam '86 with Billy Graham
1987	Writes *The Catholic People*
1988	Founds the Gallup International Institute
1992	Writes *The Saints Among Us*
2000	Writes *The Next Spirituality: Finding God in the 21st Century*

Brenda Salter McNeil

RECONCILIATION

A Prophetic Message to a Fractured Church

LEARN: Nothing this side of heaven is like being radically loved by someone racially different. Globalization is happening at a breathtaking pace. We need leaders with the agility to foster reconciliation between diverse communities.

SUCCEED: Be a bridge builder by building complementary partnerships with people from diverse cultures.

Sitting in my car in a grocery store parking lot, reflecting on six years of life in New York City and the enormous struggle over racial realities, I began to weep. I had just finished reading *Roots* by Alex Haley. His book captures the essence of the African journey to America—the suffering, the shedding of innocent blood and the separation created by slavery. It gave me the historical context to understand my experience in New York City, where racial barriers make crosscultural relationships difficult, even in the church.

At the close of my academic program at Trinity Evangelical Divinity School, I wrote a final paper entitled "The Response of the White Church to the Black Community." I worked with Dr. Bruce Fields. At the time, he was the only African American faculty member at Trinity. I asked white Christians to identify the cultural contributions of African Americans to the broader culture from a range of ten possibilities, including science, art, economics and music. The results were stunning to me. The only contributions they could identify were sports and music. They saw African Americans almost exclusively as *entertainers*. I realized then that Christians in different ethnic communities were completely uninformed of the spiritual and cultural histories of other ethnic groups.

The paper concluded with an appeal to the body of Christ to work toward what John Stott called "God's new society," the title of his book exposing Paul's letter to the Ephesian church. This new society would be marked by a commitment to *make every effort to keep the unity of the church*. Unity needs to be rooted in commitment to one another, a shared spiritual life and active efforts toward justice.

I grew up in a context with dual prejudice—against Native Americans and African Americans. My personal turning point came in 1984 after moving to New York City. With no place to live and a wife who was five months pregnant, I didn't know where to turn. At that desperate moment in our lives, we were taken in by an African American pastor. The Caesar family became a second family to us, and they taught us a powerful truth: nothing this side of heaven is like being radically loved by someone racially different.

Eight years later, in 1992, I met Brenda Salter McNeil. We were both part of an Urbana 1993 planning team. She had been invited by Dan Harrison to lead prayer at the conference, and I had been invited to co-lead an evening of prayer with her.

Working with McNeil that year was an enormous privilege. She was the only African American on our team, and I was impressed by her spirit of generosity. Already a gifted speaker and leader, she could have been protective of her ideas. But she was not. Instead, she was a learner and an encourager. Working with her is one of my professional highlights of the last thirty years. Working in a complementary relationship—female and male, black and white—was a powerful experience.

McNeil has emerged as one of the leading global voices on racial justice. She spoke at Cape Town 2010, the Lausanne Conference in South Africa, before leaders of two hundred nations, and at the 2011 Global Leadership Summit that involved more than 100,000 leaders. As one of the world's most gifted preachers, she has faithfully carried the torch of John Perkins, the "Moses" of the Reconciliation Movement.

In 2004, McNeil coauthored a book with Rick Richardson, a mutual colleague. *The Heart of Racial Justice* is an important handbook on matters related to the reconciliation of racial and ethnic communities. In the book, they describe the event that motivated me to start the concerts of prayer movement in New York City. Richardson had led a concert of prayer at Moody Memorial Church in downtown Chicago in 1987, and wrote the following:

> The group that met for prayer represented eleven different denominations, including Lutheran, Methodist, Episcopalian, Baptist and Pentecostal. The more than twelve hundred people who gathered for prayer were black, white, Latino, Native American, Asian and international. This diverse group of people held two things in common: a commitment to the lordship of Christ and a dedication to reach the city with the gospel. These people experienced a unity with one another that honored their different ethnicities and races in a way that was rare in our world.[1]

A year later, I held a concert of prayer in New York City. Since then it has attracted 200,000 participants from two thousand churches. After twenty-five years, it continues to be a sign of hope for our city. What is happening in New York is much the same as the original Chicago event.

DEFINING MOMENTS

McNeil grew up in Trenton, New Jersey, during the sixties and seventies. She lived in an immigrant community alongside Hungarian and Polish families. "My earliest crosscultural experiences were connected to food," McNeil said. "My dad really enjoyed the kielbasa from the local restaurants. We loved Polish and Italian food."[2]

McNeil was plunged into the world of multiethnicity as a sixteen-year-old camp counselor for the Reading and Recreation Program. Dorothy Katz, a Jewish philanthropist, created the program to bring together children from diverse backgrounds to participate in a summer reading program. Katz saw this as an opportunity to inspire young people to excel academically and to build crosscultural understanding. She also believed that theater would help break down racial prejudices, so she made it possible for young people in New Jersey to attend Broadway plays in New York City. Katz was sensitive to victims of ethnic stereotypes due to her own Jewish identity.

McNeil recalls that many African Americans in the seventies had militant attitudes toward white people. Going on a camping weekend with Outward Bound for the program made her aware of her own racism. "We participated in a survival exercise with other counselors from different ethnic backgrounds," said McNeil. "I will never forget struggling to climb a wall when Danny Katz reached out and pulled me up. Something in my heart began to break—it was the beginning of my own racial reconciliation journey."[3]

McNeil had grown up in a small black church led by Pastor Irene Beatrice Locks. Locks had experienced the trauma of seeing her son killed and of going through divorce when her husband did not want to attend a church where his wife was the pastor. Yet

Locks still felt called to lead the church. McNeil's faith was shaped by watching her godly, sacrificial life.

At the age of nineteen, McNeil got involved with a Bible study at Rutgers University and became part of a growing community of African Americans who had a radical faith commitment. Every Friday night they met for a Bible study that quickly grew to involve more than two hundred students. When they outgrew their meeting space, they migrated to the campus chapel.

The group was committed to evangelism, and it became the largest campus group at Rutgers. Their spiritual passion sparked a revival on campus. McNeil's faith deepened as she studied Scripture and shared her faith on campus.

Upon graduation from Rutgers, McNeil worked as a speech pathologist near her home in Trenton. In that position, she observed that many young African American children were being mislabeled as slow learners due to a fundamental injustice in the testing system that rated children based on their style of test taking rather than their knowledge or aptitude for learning.

McNeil worked with one other African American speech pathologist whose name was Bobby Smith. During the time that McNeil worked with him, he and his wife, Sharon, lost a child. In consoling their family, McNeil witnessed to Sharon, who became a Christian. "I felt called to do this," McNeil said, and this new sense of calling caused her to question whether she should be doing something different with her life.

Emerging in McNeil was the desire to influence people spiritually through evangelism and the pursuit of justice. This new direction led her to enroll at Fuller Theological Seminary in California, where she earned a Master of Divinity. At Fuller, she was influenced by the depth of commitment she witnessed in Roberta Hestenes in the area of Christian formation and discipleship. She discovered her calling as a preacher in a homiletics class taught by Dr. Ian Pitt Watson.[4]

In 1984, while finishing her degree, McNeil interned with InterVarsity at Occidental College. The college chaplain, Doug Gregg, had earned his Master of Divinity from Yale and his Ph.D. from the University of Southern California. Despite his academic achievement, however, he seemed to be wrestling spiritually. McNeil and the InterVarsity students began praying for him. Mike Flynn, an Episcopal priest active with Inter-Varsity, led Gregg to make a faith commitment to Christ. Gregg in turn allowed the college chapel to be turned into a meeting space for InterVarsity.

McNeil served students at Occidental and Pasadena City College until 1991. "Very few African American students were involved with InterVarsity," she noted. "The African American community had a very different understanding of leadership."[5] Realizing the need for some kind of reconciliation laboratory, she teamed with InterVarsity in 1986 to lead the Pasadena Urban Project. In 1990, she became codirector of the Chicago Urban Project.

McNeil began to preach on Christian college campuses in the mid-eighties. As her reputation grew, her opportunities to preach on larger stages increased. McNeil spoke and led sessions at the Urbana Mission Conferences in 1993, 1996, 2000, 2003 and 2006, and she spoke at national conferences for Youth Specialties, National Pastors Convention, Christian Community Development Association, Exponential and Catalyst to thousands of leaders. Her platform became even larger when she spoke at Cape Town 2010 and the 2011 Global Leadership Summit.

McNeil's primary influence is through her message and her mentoring. In a 2006 article in *Christianity Today,* she quoted Billy Graham, who once told David Frost, "Racial and ethnic hostility is the foremost social problem facing our world today."[6] In the same article, McNeil cites the following statistics about our changing world:

1. Ethnic minorities have doubled their share of the U.S. population since 1950.

2. According to the U.S. Census Bureau's projections, almost all the growth in U.S. population over the next 50 years will come from ethnic minorities, primarily Asian and Hispanic.

3. Shortly after 2050, non-Hispanic whites will become a minority in the United States.[7]

She warns that "we are entering a postmodern era marked, among other things, by a loss of confidence in the Western, scientific worldview." The AIDS epidemic has raised doubts that "diseases will readily yield to our technical prowess."[8]

Calling for crosscultural reconciliation. Urging Christians to practice what Scripture teaches about being reconciled to one another in Christ, McNeil writes, "We need African Christians to teach us how to preach the gospel in power."[9] As an African American woman in a position of global influence, she has a unique perspective on the world and the church. This makes her an extraordinary interpreter of culture. For more than twenty-five years, she has demonstrated the spiritual and cultural agility to navigate the diverse realities of the white church, black church and international church.

McNeil and colleagues like Rick Richardson have demonstrated the courage to wade into the very difficult and dangerous cultural land mines of the church. To the black church, they say, "Extending forgiveness is an absolutely essential act for people who have been sinned against."[10] To the white community, McNeil and Richardson write, "White Americans have benefited economically, educationally, politically and socially from the actions of their ancestors."[11]

McNeil carries forward the legacy of John Perkins, who cofounded the Christian Community Development Association with Wayne Gordon. Perkins, now over eighty years old, has influenced McNeil and others to articulate the message to an emerging generation of leaders.

On the unique role of the African American church, McNeil writes, "If African Americans ever gained a sense of our global significance we would view racial and ethnic hostilities around the world as opportunities for prophetic leadership. There are people all around the world who are waiting for us to come and share our unique perspective."[12]

McNeil affirms that the message of Jesus is for all people of all cultures for all time. This is true of those who have suffered the genocide in Rwanda and chronic poverty in Haiti. One of the great themes of world history has been the suffering of people of African descent. She emphasizes the interdependence of the body of Christ and warns against identifying first and foremost with our own ethnic community. She writes, "The message of Jesus is that anyone who identifies more with their family, their culture or their ethnic heritage is not worthy of Christ."[13]

Calling for leaders in crosscultural reconciliation. The centerpiece of McNeil's message is the urgent need for leaders with intercultural competencies to engage in reconciliation. Using the geographic sequence outlined by Jesus in Acts 1:8, she writes:

> As we lead the church into a global future we have to start in our own Jerusalem where we face our own bigotry and ethnocentrism. Judea represents people who live near us but come from a different subculture—like those from different denominations and political parties. Samaria represents the hostile places—where sex trafficking and environmental injustice takes place. The Ends of the Earth—those are the places where the greatest suffering and spiritual need exists. We need God to do something supernatural like He did at Pentecost to give us the ability to cross through the cultural sound barriers of our world.[14]

Intercultural leadership is needed more than ever in the United States, where 90 percent of people worship with others who look like themselves. The racial divide in the church is one of the most damaging limitations to the corporate witness of the church.

Wherever our faith fails to transcend ethnicity, we lose many of the next generation. Some immigrant churches experience a 90 percent attrition rate among their children if the church fails to develop a faith that transcends their immigrant culture.

According to some estimates, 10,000 congregations in the U.S. are non-English-speaking. In New York City more than 2,500 Hispanic churches reside alongside thousands of diverse Asian churches.

Inspiring others toward crosscultural influence. McNeil's message has been picked up by her students. Doug Schaupp, Urban Project alumnus, and Paula Harris cowrote *Being White: Finding Our Place in a Multiethnic World.*[15] The book wrestles with the mistakes of the white church while recognizing its contributions to the world.

Kevin Blue, another Urban Project alumnus, serves on the staff of Church of the Redeemer in Los Angeles. An African American, he became involved with InterVarsity and has served nationally as a teacher, trainer and consultant. Blue has focused on leadership development in the church with an emphasis on economic and cultural concerns. He has written two books, *Faith on the Edge* (coauthored) and *Practical Justice.*

VISION

McNeil calls for a robust spiritual vision to address the challenges of racial divides. She writes, "Racial and ethnic problems are too immense to be addressed with spiritual anemia and cynicism."[16]

To move toward personal, spiritual and social transformation, McNeil and Richardson suggest four steps:

1. Crosscultural worship—recognizing the impact of surrendering ourselves to God;

2. Embracing our true selves—doing a self-diagnostic on our own cultural posture;

3. Denouncing the powers and principalities—being awakened to the dark spiritual forces at work in us and the world; and

4. Ongoing partnerships—engaging in crosscultural friendships and efforts within diverse communities.[17]

As McNeil looks to the future she sees the need for churches to embrace a more holistic model of ministry and partnership. The model needs to move beyond the simplistic and individualistic approaches that churches have used to address community needs. She envisions people being equipped to understand how systems and social structures work—and how people of faith can be change agents in those systems.

McNeil urges churches to move beyond the dichotomy of piety and social engagement. In an age of rapid globalization, we need to see the "opportunity of Pentecost" as God brings people to our cities, communities and churches.

She challenges listeners to gauge their biblical identity across the cultural barriers of their "Jerusalem, Judea, Samaria and the ends of the earth." She also challenges her audience to do something specific as a next step. McNeil invites other leaders to build bridges with people who are different and to enter into their worlds: "The message and lifestyle of reconciliation requires immersion into the spiritual, cultural, geographic and economic realities of others."[18]

LEADER APPLICATION

- Whom is God inviting you to radically love who is racially different from you?

- What can you do to create a greater degree of awareness between diverse communities in your city (e.g., ethnic food dinners, pulpit exchanges, community celebrations)?

A prayer . . .

Jesus,

Help me to cross the "racial sound barrier" by listening to the heart cries of those who are different from me. Give me the courage to travel to be present with others in the communities where they live.

BRENDA SALTER MCNEIL'S MAJOR LIFE EVENTS

1971	Begins journey of racial justice under the influence of Dorothy Katz and the Outward Bound program
1974-1977	Attends Rutgers University and sees impact of Scripture and evangelism on campus
1981	Attends Fuller Theological Seminary and discovers preaching gift
1984	Joins InterVarsity and develops Urban Project
1993-2006	Speaks at five Urbana conferences
2004	Publishes *The Heart of Racial Justice* with Rick Richardson
2008	Receives the Maggie Sloan Crawford Legacy Award for her leadership in the arena of racial justice
2010	Speaks at Cape Town 2010, the Lausanne Congress in South Africa
2011	Speaks at the Global Leadership Summit

Alan and Katherine Barnhart

OBEDIENCE

The Global Impact of a Young Married Couple's Decision Made Twenty-Five Years Ago

LEARN: Surrender your resources to God while you are young. Make lifestyle decisions that allow you to be generous.

SUCCEED: Live simply. Be generous. Invest your resources in places where God is at work.

It was June 2011 when Katherine Barnhart and I were attending the Halftime cohort cohosted by the New York City Leadership Center, Halftime and Redeemer City to City. The purpose of the cohort was to connect leaders with their passion and calling as they consider the second "half" of their life.

In the midst of the cohort, I asked Barnhart if I could include her and her husband, Alan, in this writing project. "You have a great story regarding generosity and a lifestyle commitment," I said.

She agreed to participate, so I traveled to Memphis in August 2011 to conduct an interview. The Barnharts met me at the airport on a Sunday night. Over a barbecue dinner we discovered our many common links, one being Pradeep Ayer, the missions pastor at their church in Memphis. My wife and I had worked with Pradeep in Bihar, India, in 1983. We also had common InterVarsity roots, experiences at the Urbana Missions Conferences and involvement with the Lausanne Congress.

I stayed in their home and met four of their six children. Their lives were full with the needs of family and the demands of running a large company, yet their lifestyle was simple. Katherine was getting ready to travel to meetings in Chicago, Dallas and Singapore in the next two weeks. Nevertheless, she and Alan spent significant time with me. We talked over dinner, met for a formal interview early in the morning and spent additional time at Alan's office, where I interviewed him.[1]

Nicholas, their oldest son, is a clear-headed young man. A third-generation Barnhart working in the family business, he is much like his dad, having become an engineer at the University of Tennessee. While hosting me for lunch, he asked, "What has most surprised you in the writing of your book?" My biggest surprise, I told him, was seeing the important role of mentors and catalytic events in people's lives.[2]

His parents are no exception.

DEFINING MOMENTS

Alan and Katherine both grew up in the Methodist church. "I have always loved going to church and have always loved God," said Katherine. "I showed my love for God by trying so hard to be good. It wasn't until I picked up a Bible at my grandmother's home at age ten and couldn't put it down I realized that Christ was asking me to respond to him personally. I heard the gospel clearly, simply and in a way that I could understand in the eighth grade. I made a firm commitment to Christ in response to this good news."

Alan's experience was different. "I believed I had always been a Christian until the day before I actually became one," he explained. "I was attending a Young Life camp as a sixteen-year-old. One day the camp focus was on the cross of Christ and the necessity of his death. I realized how far short I fell of God's standards. The next day the theme was transferring our trust to Christ. That's when my faith became real."[3]

Alan arrived at the University of Tennessee to study engineering in 1979. He became active with InterVarsity. Katherine came as a freshman in 1982, and the two ended up in the same IVCF Bible study. As a senior, Alan viewed Katherine as a little sister. And Katherine came to love Alan as an older, spiritual brother. "He was the first young man I had ever met who was more spiritually mature [than I was]," she said.

While in college Alan learned about the Ethiopian famine (1982-1984). He also read Ron Sider's book *Rich Christians in an Age of Hunger,* which made him have second thoughts about attending a ski weekend with friends. "How can we live this lifestyle while people are starving?" he asked himself. He decided to cancel his ski trip and donate the cost of it—$350—to famine relief. He influenced several friends to do the same, and together they donated $2,000. The seed of financial obedience had taken root.

After graduation Alan returned to the University of Tennessee to participate in a weekend InterVarsity retreat. When the weekend was over, Alan wrote a letter to Katherine expressing his interest in a relationship. In the letter he said, "Just let me know."

As Katherine was weighing what to do next, her dad heard her heart for Alan and encouraged her to respond to him. He slapped a ten-dollar bill on the table for a long-distance call and said, "Call the man."

After the two dated for a few weekends, Katherine transferred to Memphis State University to be closer to Alan. They were engaged in December, and two weeks later they attended the Urbana Missions Conference. Alan participated in the donor track, and Katherine participated in the student track. The preaching of Elisabeth Elliot and

Billy Graham challenged them to go anywhere that God would send them. Both felt a strong interest in going to the Muslim world as tent-makers. "We wanted to go overseas right away," Katherine said, "but were counseled to be married for a year before leaving the States."

During the first year of Alan and Katherine's marriage, Alan's parents announced that they had decided to leave their company and sail around the world. They offered Alan and his brother, Eric, the opportunity to start their own business and to continue the existing operation so the families of the ten employees working for them wouldn't lose their livelihood. Katherine felt that they should proceed with their plan to serve as tentmakers in a closed country as missionaries. Alan's reaction was different. "I felt more gifted in the area of business than in ministry," he said. "I wanted to start a new kind of company."[4]

Alan suggested an idea to Katherine that seemed like a way to accomplish both ambitions. They would start a new kind of company and invest the profits into missions. Katherine was not convinced. They kept voting on what to do, and the vote always ended in a one-to-one tie. Eventually Katherine relented. "I gave Alan my vote as a proxy," she said. Not surprisingly, he decided to stay. Convinced that the Holy Spirit could accomplish in Alan what she could not, Katherine left the outcome with God. "I believed that Alan would be swallowed by a whale and spit out where God wanted us to serve," she said in jest.

During the previous two years, Alan had read and systematized Bible verses about topics related to the poor, wealth and giving. He discovered two core principles. One had to do with stewardship, believing that God owns everything. The second was a warning against the dangers of wealth.

Katherine had her own concerns about the dangers of wealth. "I saw so many women who spent everything—their time, emotions, talents and treasures—on themselves. They had nothing left to give," she said. "I did not want to be like that."

Alan and his brother, Eric, a mechanical genius, became partners in the new company. Both couples committed to a "finish-line lifestyle," in which a family determines what they can live on as though they were missionaries themselves and contributes the rest of their earnings into missions. In the first year, Alan and Katherine took a salary equivalent to what a staff person with Campus Crusade or InterVarsity would earn.

Barnhart Construction Company had been started in 1969 by Alan's parents. The new company started in 1986 as Barnhart Crane and Rigging Company. At the age of twenty-five, Alan had solidified his philosophy of wealth that would shape his company and family for the next twenty-five years. The Barnharts were committed to two parameters: to not increase their lifestyle as the company grew, and to give away as much money to missions as they could.

As the new company started, Katherine entered a period of uncertainty. "Alan was working one hundred hours a week," she said. "I was struggling with the decision to start the new company."

Refusing to let her circumstances keep her from reaching the unreached, she connected with a local Southeast Asian refugee community. Working with enormous passion, she grew the ministry of four people into one involving several hundred.

In 1987, Nicholas, their first child, was born. Over the next thirteen years, five more children were added—Nathan, Janie, Kepler, Marah and Noah, and Sarah, lost at birth. Two of these were added through adoption. Katherine invested her life in the children, homeschooling them through childhood. Katherine said, "God gifted us with each of these children into our lives and built this family."

One of their first decisions involving the new company was to create GROVE (God's Resources Operating Very Effectively) as a way to steward resources, if there were any. GROVE involves employees in the giving decisions. "Our desire is to keep personal pride out of the giving process and share the joy of giving. So we involve team members of the company and their spouses in the giving process and make decisions as a group. We started as a group of six, and now it's almost 50 people."[5] In its first year GROVE gave away $25,000.

The company had several defining moments. In 1990, it bought its biggest competitor. In 1992, it established its first branch in Decatur, Alabama. Then it entered the 1997-2000 power boom years, which Alan characterizes as having "lots of opportunity, lots of people and lots of problems." As the company began to grow in the late 1990s, it experienced a number of accidents. "We move heavy equipment," said Alan, "and there has always been a need to be very careful." So in 2002, the company established a senior leadership team to draft statements regarding company values, mission and purpose.

Fueled by several innovations—including the slide system, multipurpose pumps, tri-block, quad block, tip stick and dolly transporter—largely the result of Eric Barnhart's genius and ingenuity, the company has become the largest of its type in the United States.

The company works primarily in five markets, including wind, fossil fuel and nuclear power. The wind industry opened up in 2003 and created $100 million in revenue. The company has created two thousand wind turbines. Between 2004 and 2008 the company experienced a fivefold growth—from $50 million to $250 million.

As the company grew, so did its ability to give away large amounts of funding. Joye Allen, who serves as Alan's administrator and also as the administrator for GROVE, showed me a soon-to-be-released video about GROVE. It tells the story of employees who are motivated by their work because they not only earn a living but also help others.[7] Joye recognizes her employment as "holy work." "We are giving back to the Lord what he has entrusted to us," she said. "We have our biases philanthropically to give money internationally, especially in the 10/40 window where Christianity is the most marginalized."[8]

COMPANY PURPOSE, MISSION AND VALUES

Purpose Statement

The purpose of Barnhart Crane and Rigging Company is to glorify God by providing an opportunity for his people to use their skills and gifts in his service through constructive work, personal witness and ministry funding.

Mission Statement

Barnhart Crane and Rigging Company will continuously improve to be the best heavy lift and heavy transport company.

Core Values

Safety. Barnhart Crane and Rigging Company will invest the time and money necessary to ensure the safety of our employees, customers, vendors and the general public. We will further protect property and the environment.

Quality Service. Barnhart Crane and Rigging Company will train our employees and monitor our processes to ensure consistent excellence and an appropriate effort to meet the needs of our customers.

Continuous Improvement. Barnhart Crane and Rigging Company will evaluate and critique all areas of our company with an eye for improvement.

Innovation. Barnhart Crane and Rigging Company will be proactive in creating better methods and tools to meet the needs of our customers.

Fairness. Barnhart Crane and Rigging Company will strive to be honest and fair to all employees, vendors and customers.

Profit with a Purpose. Barnhart Crane and Rigging Company will attempt to make profits and will invest the profit to expand the company and to meet the needs of others (physically, mentally, spiritually).[6]

The company had modest but steady growth from 1986 to 2004. The largest period of growth began in 2005 and peaked in 2008. The income forecast for 2011 was $230 million. The giving of GROVE jumped almost eight times from 2004 to 2005 and reached the philanthropic milestone of giving away almost $1 million each month beginning in 2008. To date, the total invested is about $70 million with $15 million still in the account.

As the children grew and became more independent, Katherine wanted a more active role in global missions. In 2000 she was invited to join the board of The Jesus Film Project. "I was so surprised to be invited into this level of leadership with mission agency leaders," she said. "I saw myself primarily as a mother raising her children. I felt like an Esther sitting at the table with these mission leaders."[9]

Since 2000, Katherine has served as a board member or adviser for InterVarsity, Every Tribe Every Nation (Scripture Project), The JESUS Film Project, Memphis Leadership Foundation and World Relief. Alan serves on the board of Student Mobilization.

The demands of work, parenting and mission leadership make it easy for Alan and Katherine to drift into parallel lives. So they work hard to create shared experiences. Often it involves global travel with their family. Their children have experienced missions in a variety of ways. Nicholas has been to twenty countries and served as a steward at Cape Town 2010. Katherine chuckled when she said, "Nicholas is the prototype for all of my children."

Katherine summarizes the major themes of their lives and marriage. "We have learned to be content not because of who we are but because of Whose we are," she says. "We choose to live counterculturally and not spend money unnecessarily. We see our lives as being dependent on Scripture."[10]

CONSEQUENTIAL IMPACT

Barnhart Crane and Rigging has received the Specialized Carrier Job of the Year Award eighteen times for innovation and safe per-

formance. The company also has acquired eleven other companies, expanded to twenty-one branches across the country, and
grown to nine hundred employees from the original ten in 1986.

But for the Barnhart family, the success of the business is not measured by its size or by the amount of money it takes in; it's measured
by what it gives. As a result, the employees at Barnhart consider their
work to be more than a job; it's a mission. By connecting profession to
philanthropy, work is elevated. "The reward for good work is more
work," said Alan. "That is how the company has grown steadily over
the past twenty-five years. We give our employees a God-sized vision."

Employees are invited to travel to develop relationships with
company-funded ministries. These partnerships with mission
agencies have helped the rural poor in China as well as young
people living near the company, which is located in one of the
toughest neighborhoods in Memphis. GROVE has partnered with
a local ministry to provide after-school programming and leadership development for hundreds of inner-city youth in Memphis.
"We have helped to adopt four public schools and are seeing many
young people go on to college," said Joye Allen.[11]

The philanthropy focuses on evangelism, church planting, discipleship, leadership training and ministry to the poorest of the
poor. Over thirty Barnhart employees are actively involved in elements of the giving process.

The Barnharts' children also are adopting their parents' values.
They all have a vibrant faith. In particular, Nicholas talked about
his interest in missions. He considers it a privilege to work at the
family business because of its high value on missions. Nathan in-
vests in the lives of young men as a Young Life leader. Kepler, a
younger brother, is active in the Young Life group on his high
school campus. The other children are active in First Evangelical
Church, the local church the family attends in Memphis.

The Barnharts have developed a philosophy of giving that is articulated in this statement: "Our giving is HIPPP: We give humbly,

intentionally, in partnership, personally and proactively."[12] The GROVE board has set up very clear guidelines on the priorities of their philanthropy. They involve their employees as "champions" for specific mission efforts that they want to consider investing in.

VISION

Alan and Katherine want to see a generation of young people who take God at his word. Alan believes it is strategic to invest in young entrepreneurs. "They can be influenced and encouraged to adopt a 'finish-line lifestyle' that follows what we have learned for twenty-five years," he said.

The Barnharts also want to see improved crosscultural communication skills within the church. They see the enormous economic and spiritual divide between nations, and the need to effectively navigate the divide is increasingly important.

Twenty-five years ago a newlywed couple established a vision for a finish-line lifestyle that shaped their commitment to family and work. As a result, hundreds of thousands of lives have been improved in this world and changed for eternity.

LEADER APPLICATION

- What would it take to create a finish-line lifestyle for you, your family or your business?
- How would this increase your personal, family and organizational philanthropic potential?
- How is your life mission and professional calling integrated and connected to God's larger purposes?

A prayer . . .

Jesus,

Give us a clean lens to see what obedience looks like. Help us to align our resources with our hearts.

ALAN AND KATHERINE BARNHART'S
MAJOR LIFE EVENTS

1984	Alan and Katherine attend Urbana 1984 Missions Conference
1985	Alan and Katherine marry
1986	Barnhart Crane and Rigging is founded
1990	Barnhart Crane and Rigging purchases largest competitor
2000	Katherine Barnhart joins boards of InterVarsity and the Jesus Film
2002	Establishes company values, mission and purpose statements
2005	GROVE group gives away $5 million in funding
2011	GROVE group has given away more than $70 million cumulatively

Bob Doll

STRATEGY

Leveraging One's Professional Calling to Influence the World

LEARN: Become a credible witness by being the best in your industry.

SUCCEED: Leverage your influence through strategic partnerships and strategic philanthropy.

For more than thirty years, Bob Doll has been providing U.S. financial market analysis. He understands the interplay between national financial health and global spiritual realities. At the Cape Town 2010 Lausanne meeting, he presented a seminar on spiritual and financial global trends, explaining the trajectory of the two and highlighting the enormous changes in China.

China's economy is predicted to grow as high as seventy trillion dollars by 2050, compared to forty trillion dollars in the United States. In 2005, China had an estimated 111 million Christians. Only the United States and Brazil have more. If estimates are correct, the Christian population will grow to 218 million by 2050, making it second only to the United States. China has both the fastest-growing economy and the fastest-growing Christian population in the world.

By 2050, Asia, Africa and Latin America will be home to more than 70 percent of the world's Christians—up from 22 percent in 1900 (see table 13.1). Fourteen of the twenty-one fastest-growing financial markets in the world are located in Asia and Latin America (where the annual increase in GDP is 4.5 percent).[1]

Table 13.1

Country	Percentage of Christians in 1900	Percentage of Christians in 2050
Asia	2	20
Africa	9	29
Latin America	11	22

At Cape Town 2010, Doll and his wife, Leslie, were participating in the Global Executive Leadership Forum (GELF), an effort to connect impassioned, Christ-centered marketplace leaders with one another. I met Doll at one of the receptions. Later that week he and I had breakfast with Mark Reynolds, a colleague from Redeemer City to City. Prior to that, Doll and Tim Keller had been spending time together. Little by little we discovered that we had overlapping passions and interests, so we started to explore the possibility of collaborating on the New York City Movement Project.

My next meeting with Doll took place with Tim Keller in February 2011 at the Redeemer offices in Manhattan. We were joined by Lloyd Reeb and Bob Durfey of Halftime, a movement that connects midlife Christian marketplace leaders who are deciding how best to use their remaining years.[2] We met to discuss a strategic alliance between Halftime and the New York City Movement Project. Our goal was to connect Christian marketplace leaders to their future calling in the context of a city-reaching movement.

We agreed to launch this strategy in June 2011 in New York City.

I met Leslie Doll, Bob's wife, in May 2011 at Bob's BlackRock Investment offices in Princeton, New Jersey. She and Bob met on a blind date in the 1980s. She had graduated from Southern Methodist University and was working on Wall Street. The Dolls have three children, two in college and one at home. They are active in the Westerly Road Church, where Bob has played the organ and led the choir for twenty years.[3]

DEFINING MOMENTS

Doll spent his early childhood in northeast Philadelphia. When he was in the sixth grade, his family moved to Bucks County, Pennsylvania, where he spent the rest of his childhood. Doll has lived his entire life within a fifty-mile radius of Princeton, New Jersey. He attended Lehigh University and graduated with degrees in economics and mathematics.

His spiritual roots are in the Methodist church, but his faith didn't fully develop until he went to college. "While I attended the Wharton School of Management, I attended Tenth Presbyterian Church in Philadelphia, where my faith became very solid," Doll said. Later, while living in New York City, his faith grew under the preaching of Dr. Donald Hubbard at Calvary Baptist Church in Manhattan.[4] After Doll finished his academic training, his career had a meteoric rise, beginning in 1980 at Citigroup and continuing at Oppenheimer, Merrill Lynch and BlackRock.

For ten years, Doll lived in Princeton, New Jersey, and commuted to New York City. Eventually the three-hour daily commute took its toll. He had a young family and was feeling the strain of the long days. He prayed, "God, if you will open an employment opportunity to bring my worlds together, I will seize it." The answer came in the form of an offer from Merrill Lynch. He was invited to take a position in Princeton that would save three hours of commuting. "We want you to take those three hours from each day and give one to yourself, one to your family, and one to the company," the interviewer said. "In retrospect," says Bob, "the company took all three hours plus two for themselves."

In 2001, Doll became the president of Merrill Lynch Investment Management, one of the world's ten largest investment management firms. From 2001 to 2006, Doll's division generated nearly 10 percent of Merrill Lynch's revenues.

Doll describes his responsibilities at Merrill Lynch: "I gave oversight to 2,500 employees and was asked to fix our profit and loss ratios, fix investment performance and to turn the division around. My first assignment was to cut $700 million in expenses."[5]

After five years at Merrill Lynch, Doll concluded that he was married to his job. "I realized that over an eight-year period—from 1997 to 2005—I had absolutely no margin in my life," he said. "I was identifying with my position in a way that was inappropriate."

This prompted Doll's second prayer: "God, help me to come down from all of this responsibility so that I have more time for other priorities in my life." The answer came in 2006 when Merrill Lynch sold Doll's division to BlackRock Investment Management, now the largest investment firm in the world. Doll became the chief equity strategist at BlackRock, where he and his team are responsible to manage $28 billion. But the change in assignment involved less responsibility and fewer time pressures.

In 2009, Doll met Doug Birdsall, executive director of Lausanne. Birdsall traveled the world to mobilize people from two hundred nations for Cape Town 2010. Birdsall invited Doll to participate as an attendee and as an investor. "Leslie and I had decided to invest $100,000 in Lausanne," Doll recalls. "Birdsall challenged us to add a zero to our commitment."[6] Doll's million-dollar investment and involvement attracted other investors to sponsor the fifteen-million-dollar Congress.

The answer to Doll's second prayer is ongoing. As a couple, he and Leslie have become involved in joint opportunities. Together they are involved in a Halftime cohort, where they are concentrating on listening to God and hearing his direction for their life together. In his career, Bob has followed the recommendation of Jim Lane, a former Goldman Sachs partner and founder of the New Canaan Society, who advised Doll to stay in his profession. Lane said, "You have far more credibility sitting in the chair as a working leader than as an ex-leader sitting in the chair." Doll agrees. He knows that being good at what he does gives him credibility.

CONSEQUENTIAL IMPACT

Doll is one of the world's leading voices on financial markets. According to Priyan Fernando, executive vice president of Global Business Solutions at American Express, "Bob Doll is the final word on the markets."[7]

Doll appears regularly on television shows and provides market analysis for *USA Today, The Wall Street Journal* and a host of other publications. His position, reputation and outspoken faith open doors for him to witness to colleagues and speak to Christian M.B.A. students about the integration of faith and work.

Doll recounted a conversation he had with two BlackRock executives, the president and CEO, both of whom are Jewish. These top corporate leaders were puzzled by a Scripture they heard at a Jewish wedding. They were amazed when Doll clarified the meaning for them based on his own faith in a Jewish Messiah.

In recent years, Doll has spoken to Christian fellowships on twelve campuses. He has remarkable influence on aspiring financial leaders who are eager to follow the trail that Doll has blazed for thirty years.

In a talk entitled "Our Story of Victory in Him," Doll addresses the theme of being a worshiper as an aspect of vocational calling. "As your eternal perspective increases, your worldly perspective will decrease," Doll says. "When you decrease your focus on completing and accomplishing things, you will love people more."[8]

When interviewed by David Miller at the Greenwich Leadership Forum, Doll said, "By seeking God's will we could find our purpose on Earth. When we find a place where our interest and skill set intersect with a need and opportunity, our ability to serve could be a sweet mix. We share our faith through the authenticity of our lifestyles."[9]

Strategic influence. Philanthropy is a big part of Doll's strategy for making an impact. He and Leslie made a sizable contribution for the construction of a chapel at the University Medical Center of Princeton. They also were involved in the architectural design of the chapel. Doll said, "Leslie and I are pleased to make this gift, knowing that a special place of prayer, of refuge and of celebration will be built at the new hospital."[10] Richard White, the director of religious ministries at the medical center, said of the Doll gift, "Patients, family members and hospital staff can be found in the chapel night or day. I sometimes call it 'The Soul' of the system. We are grateful that attention is being paid to the chapel in the new facility."[11]

GIVEN THE ENORMITY OF THE 2008 FINANCIAL CRISIS, WHAT IS YOUR PERSPECTIVE ON HOW WE SHOULD LOOK AT MONEY?

"Money is a tool, a medium of exchange," as economists like to say. It is not to be a god, nor is it something we can totally depend on (we used to say, "as dependable as a U.S. dollar"). And yet we need money to live and to accumulate wealth. The question is, for what purpose? In my view, God may be "shaking the nations" in this multi-year test of economies and markets in part because of our excesses (greed, too much debt, love of money). I hope and pray it causes all of us—believers and nonbelievers alike—to turn to him.

In addition to their philanthropy, the Dolls participate in other strategic ways. Leslie Doll has developed a passion for Christian women in the Muslim world, so she and Bob have joined the Strategic Resource Group, a cohort of fifty partners who each contribute a significant amount over a multiyear period to invest in strategic outreach among Muslims.[12] The couple recognizes that few mission dollars are going to the Middle East.

In Egypt, Leslie participated for two weeks in a ministry for Egyptian Christians living and working in a slum in Cairo. Over a dinner meeting with Bob Buford in Dallas, her face lit up when Buford expressed interest in her passion for Middle Eastern women. Doors are opening for like-minded business leaders to address the great spiritual and humanitarian issues of our day.[13]

The Dolls also are leading the Global Executive Leadership Forum (GELF), launched at Cape Town 2010. Doug Birdsall, in his summary report on the Lausanne Biennial Leadership Meeting, wrote, "The emergence of GELF may prove to be one of the most significant developments of Cape Town 2010. . . . GELF will connect and resource business leaders of global influence who have a profound commitment to Christ and the mission of the church in the world."[14]

"Consider the recent uprisings in Egypt," Doll said. "I envision a future conference call with Egyptian Christian business leaders who may want to participate and invest in specific opportunities to assist the church in Egypt in the midst of enormous need and change."[15]

Doll also envisions the GELF leaders gathering annually to study God's Word, build community and form alliances for future strategic kingdom service.[16]

The New York City Movement Project. The Dolls have joined Redeemer City to City and the New York City Leadership Center to launch the New York City Movement Project, an initiative dedicated to influencing New York City for Christ. The project is happening in the context of an increasing spiritual presence in the city. Research commissioned in 2009 by Redeemer City to City and the New York City Leadership Center indicated that the percentage of evangelical Christians living in midtown Manhattan has tripled in twenty years (from 1 to 3 percent).

This has happened primarily through a movement of church planting and leader development initiated by Redeemer, Concerts of Prayer Greater New York and the New York City Leadership Center. If the evangelical population triples again in the next ten to twenty years, the city could reach a "tipping point."[17] When that happens, evangelical Christianity in Manhattan will influence the entire world.

"I didn't realize how important reaching 10 percent was until I saw the influence of the Christian church in Egypt," said Leslie Doll. "Egypt has a 10 percent indigenous Christian presence, and it is vastly different from other parts of the Muslim world, where it is perhaps 1 or 2 percent. Reaching 10 percent makes a crucial, culture-changing difference."[18]

The NYC Movement Project believes in a "gospel ecosystem"— an environment where diverse elements come together (e.g., church-planting movements, mission agencies and marketplace leaders) for maximum spiritual growth. Tim Keller and the Dolls bring together leaders who are at the height of influence in their respective arenas—pastoral and financial.

For every new church the church-planting alliance has nurtured through vision casting, prayer, training and funding, another two churches have emerged. By planting one hundred new churches in five years, the NYC Movement Project may see two or three times that many churches start.

The vision of the NYC Movement Project involves developing leaders in churches, nonprofit organizations and the marketplace by using trainers from the most effective organizations, such as Halftime, Willow Creek Leadership Summit and Redeemer City to City.

The final element of the NYC Movement Project is Movement Day, a one-day congress that brings together leaders from the largest cities in the United States to incubate and accelerate gospel movements in their respective cities. A gospel movement is defined as a spiritual movement that causes the growth of the Christian population to exceed the growth of the general population. It takes a city to change a culture, a gospel movement to change a city and a leader to catalyze a gospel movement.

In 2011, leaders from thirty-four states and fourteen countries attended the first Movement Day. The five-year goal is to host leaders from one hundred global cities in New York City—home of the most international church in human history. Doll says:

> I see an incredible coming together of powerful global movements like Lausanne, GELF and agencies from the United States to combine our efforts to participate in what could be a new spiritual awakening in our lifetime. I believe in the Movement Project because it is built on the foundation of a twenty-year partnership between Tim Keller and Mac Pier, along with Redeemer and Concerts of Prayer/the NYC Leadership Center. The Movement Project is also rooted in a twenty-five-year prayer movement.[19]

IF YOU WERE TO ADVISE YOUNGER MARKETPLACE PROFESSIONALS TO DO ONE THING, WHAT WOULD THAT BE—BOTH PROFESSIONALLY AND SPIRITUALLY?

I advise young leaders to live by Romans 12:2. "Do not be conformed to this world, but be transformed by the renewal of your mind, that by testing you may discern what is the will of God, what is good and acceptable and perfect" (ESV). What this has meant for me is the following:

1. *Plan your life path as diligently as you plan your career path.*

2. *Depend on God, not yourself.*

3. *Give away yourself and all you have.*

4. *Understand that it's not about you.*

5. *Develop a love for the things of the world to come.*

6. *Learn the lessons of the valley.*

7. *Live a life of worship.*

Doll is so passionate about collaboration that he provides me with his travel schedule and offers to speak to leaders in any city where he might be traveling. When a request is made for a time he would be available to speak by phone with strategic leaders, someone from Doll's office responds within a few hours of the request with six or seven times that Doll would be available.

VISION

As Doll studies the global landscape of Christianity and the national landscape of U.S. financial markets, he comes to this conclusion:

> The church in America desperately needs revival. We need to get back to the basics of seeking God in prayer and Scripture. All of the efforts that Leslie and I participate in ultimately need to bring people back to their fundamental relationship with God. In the United States and Europe, where we have had relative affluence in comparison to the rest of the world, the church is in deep decline. We believe in the basic truths of submitting ourselves to God in alignment with Romans 12:2: "be transformed by the renewing of your mind."[20]

The global church, with its rapid growth in Africa, Latin America and Asia, can serve as a catalyst to spiritual growth in America.

Doll is committed to developing strategic alliances to increase the efficiency and effectiveness of messengers proclaiming the good news of Christ around the world.

LEADER APPLICATION

- What would you need to do to become the best in your particular vocation?
- How might you leverage your influence through strategic partnerships with others in your industry?

A prayer . . .

Jesus,

I pray that you will fill me with a passion to do with excellence what you have called me to do. Help me to discover others who are like-minded about making a difference.

BOB DOLL'S MAJOR LIFE EVENTS

1980-1987	Citigroup Investment Management
1987-1999	Chief Investment Officer, Oppenheimer Funds
1999-2006	President, Merrill Lynch Investment Management
2006-	Chief Equity Strategist, BlackRock Investment
2011-	Leadership Team with Leslie Doll: Global Executive Leadership Forum, the NYC Movement Project

Jim Mellado and Steve Bell

TEAM

The Willow Creek Association Team
Ignites a Leadership Revolution

LEARN: The mutual submission of a team can unleash
power capable of changing the world.

SUCCEED: Gather smart leaders who have mutual respect for
one another and work for a larger global good.

Members of the Willow Creek Association team—Jim Mellado,
Steve Bell, Jim Becks and Dave Wright—arrived in the lobby of
the LaGuardia Marriott Hotel in July 2004. Three of the four
were seriously underdressed for a midtown Manhattan re-
ception. We had only one option—an emergency fashion run to
Sears. After purchasing three blue blazers, Jim Mellado quipped,
"I think we should ask about a 20,000-mile warranty on our
new jackets."

For the next two days, we toured, strategized and laughed our
way across New York City. It became obvious to me that this group
really enjoyed each other.

The team was in town to learn how they could provide annual, affordable and accessible leadership development for pastors and church leaders in the city. I was impressed right away by the way they worked together. Although they were leading one of the largest church movements in the world, there was no indication that any of them was concerned about who had what title. They recognized that what they could accomplish together was much greater than anything they could do individually.

DEFINING MOMENTS

Jim Mellado. Mellado's spiritual roots trace back to his great-grandfather, an itinerant Presbyterian missionary to Mexico. Both of his parents are American citizens by birth but Mexican by culture. Due to his father's job as an engineer working on construction projects in developing countries, his parents moved more than forty times in fifty-plus years of marriage. Mellado attended ten schools in twelve years before graduating from high school in Texas. He then attended Southern Methodist University before entering graduate school at Harvard, where he earned an M.B.A.

As his family traveled around the globe, Mellado worshiped in every type of church imaginable—from dirt-floor structures to magnificent, modern-day buildings. These experiences laid the foundation for him to become president of a global movement of church leaders.[1]

Mellado is an exceptional leader. In addition to cultural and educational qualifications, his inner qualities—personal piety, gentle demeanor and wisdom to match his intellect—make him uniquely suited for his position at Willow Creek Association (WCA).

Mellado is also an Olympic decathlete. He represented El Salvador in the 1988 games in Seoul, Korea, and won his group in the high jump event.

Steve Bell. I was introduced to Mellado by Steve Bell, whom I met in Washington, D.C., in 1994. I was leaving InterVarsity Christian

Fellowship staff after thirteen years, and Steve was leaving the nationally syndicated radio ministry *The Chapel of the Air* after twelve years. As associate director, he had been cohost and speaker on the broadcast, which aired daily on 450 radio stations across the U.S. and Canada. Both of us were joining Concerts of Prayer International (COPI) to work with David Bryant, the founder. Steve would serve as executive director, managing the overall ministry at the national headquarters office near Chicago. I would lead the movement in New York City. Our assignment was to stimulate the rapidly growing prayer movement in the United States.

We both left COPI in 1998, and Steve joined the executive team of WCA as an executive vice president. His assignment was to take the growing ministry of Willow Creek outside the walls of Willow. When Steve joined the team, Willow had nearly three thousand WCA member churches. Today there are more than seven thousand member churches from thirty-five countries and more than ninety denominations. Steve's leadership played a significant role in this growth. His experience at COPI added to the multiple relationships and connections he needed to make this happen.

Bell's spiritual life was shaped by his rural Ohio upbringing via godly parents, a healthy family, a positive local church experience and especially his pastor. Bell recalls Pastor McCracken's leadership: "He had a real heart and love for people and a clear vision with an intense passion for international missions, taking me on a four-week mission trip to South America in 1967, and years earlier for two weeks of service in Mexico. Because of his personal interest and focused attention in my life at strategic times, we became close friends, and he made ministry delightful."[2] McCracken's leadership style is evident in Bell—full of warmth and empty of self.

Bell and I often reflect on the leading of God in our relationship and friendship. It has been a remarkable evidence of God's choreography to see how our lives and relationships have brought leaders together. It has been a gift to connect leaders in New York City with the most dynamic Christian leadership movement in the world. We share a common vision of an enduring friendship in strategic places that accelerates the purpose of God through a well-led church.

"When we parted ways in 1998, I was very confident that our paths would come back together," Bell has said on several occasions. "It has been incredibly rewarding to see what has grown from our long-term friendship."

Willow Creek Community Church: A revolution begins. Bill Hybels started Willow Creek Community Church in 1975 after hearing a lecture on Acts 2 at Trinity College in Deerfield, Illinois. He was challenged by the radical lifestyle of early Christians who devoted themselves to the teaching of the apostles, eating together, caring for one another and sharing their possessions. Hybels wanted to start a church like that—one that would "turn irreligious people into fully devoted followers of Jesus Christ."[3]

Hybels started Willow Creek when the church in America was entering a period of troubling decline. Hybels was young, optimistic and energetic. He worked hard to find out what made people stop going to church, and based on the information he gathered, he started a different kind of church, a church that started a wave of change that rolled through congregations all across the nation.

By acting on the answers they received to one simple question—"Why don't you attend church?"—Hybels and his team defied the trend of decline. The candid answers they received fell into these categories:

- Churches always asked for money, yet nothing perceived as personally significant seemed to happen with it.
- Church services were boring and lifeless.
- Church services were predictable.
- Sermons were irrelevant to life in the "real world."
- The pastor made people feel guilty and ignorant, so they left the church feeling worse than when they entered.[4]

Willow Creek was so successful that it gained the attention of Peter Drucker, the century's leading expert on management. In 1989, Drucker featured Willow Creek in his *Harvard Business Review* article, "What Business Can Learn from Nonprofits." Drucker described the impact of organizations like the Girl Scouts, the Red Cross and Willow Creek Community Church (WCCC).[5]

During this time, Mellado was in graduate school at Harvard (1989-1991), and he was asked by a Harvard professor, Dr. Leonard A. Schlesinger, to write a case study about the rapidly growing church in the suburbs of Chicago. Mellado's project highlighted the leadership style of this life-changing organization. At the time of the 1991 study, Willow Creek had an average attendance of 14,000 people, the highest of any congregation in America. The church was raising over twelve million dollars per year and had 4,500 volunteers serving in 6,000 volunteer positions.

This was during a time, according to Mellado's research, when the number of unchurched Americans had doubled over a fourteen-year period in the eighties and nineties. Mellado saw the American church trending in the same direction as the church in Western Europe, where cathedrals are empty and Christian influence is minuscule. He concluded that America was potentially one generation away from a European non-Christian reality.[6]

Willow Creek Association. The meteoric growth of Willow Creek made other churches want to learn from it. Church leaders from all over the world asked to visit and study the model. The large number of inquiries made Hybels and other key WCCC leaders realize the need for a formal association to assist churches. He invited Mellado to join Willow Creek and help grow the start-up association. Mellado had an important decision to make. He was on a fast career track with his degree in engineering and a Harvard M.B.A. After wrestling to align his opportunities and his values, he made the decision to work for Hybels and join this new initiative that Willow Creek had launched.

Willow Creek Association got off to a bumpy start. In 1992, its first year of operation, WCA experienced a significant financial loss. Mellado was named president in its second year, and he was given very little time to get the organization on solid financial footing.

WCA "rebooted" with Mellado as president. He describes 1994 through 2005 as the "wonder years" of growth. A conference ministry was created to assist leaders in areas ranging from church leadership, preaching and children's ministry to financial stewardship and the arts.

The Leadership Summit began in 1995 as an on-site WCA event held in Willow's 4,300-seat auditorium. Within a few years this event was selling out a year in advance. To accommodate the demand, a simulcast satellite version was added in 1998 with two locations—the Dallas and San Francisco areas.

Mellado, Bell and the WCA leadership team began to study those who came to their conferences and events. They discovered that participants were entrepreneurial church planters, pioneers and leaders willing to take risks. They characterized them as voracious learners.

The big idea for WCA in the early days was to train and inspire interested church leaders with Willow's innovative ideas. This resulted in Willow-type churches being planted in cities across the U.S. and even in other countries. Influenced by the coaching of Peter Drucker, Everett Rogers and Bob Buford, WCA's leadership team saw their ministry as a network for diffusing "best practices" to other churches. They share the conviction of management experts that 16 percent of any social system is the innovators and early adopters. Results happen by influencing them, so that is the strategy they followed.[7]

In 1996, Gary Schwammlein joined WCA to oversee international operations. Schwammlein, a native German, had worked for the Monsanto Chemical Company for twenty-five years, representing the business throughout the world, including Southeast Asia, Europe and Africa. In 1994 he had heard a message from Hybels titled "The Legacy of a Leader," in which Hybels challenged listeners to consider "when is enough, enough, and when does saving become hoarding?" After leading in a Fortune 100 corporation, Schwammlein decided that he had had enough. Sixteen months later he began his position with WCA. Schwammlein believes that God had been preparing him for this position through his international marketplace career since his conversion at age twenty-nine.[8]

Under Schwammlein's leadership, the global expression of WCA and the Summit experience exploded. As of 2009, the number of Global Leadership Summit registrants, which includes many church leaders who earn less than two dollars per day, surpassed attendees in North America.

Table 14.1

WCA's Leadership Summit Attendance at Satellite Sites			
Year	North America	International	Total
1998	1,500		1,500
1999	3,282		3,282
2000	6,532		6,532
2001	7,596		7,596
2002	21,487		21,487
2003	29,601		29,601
2004	31,950		31,950
2005	39,850	14,499	43,349
2006	46,950	24,219	71,169
2007	50,270	41,367	91,637
2008	46,857	46,426	93,283
2009	45,135	56,227	101,362
2010	52,595	65,232	117,827
2011	68,529	78,000	146,529

Source: The Leadership Summit registrations at satellite sites, 1998-2011, Willow Creek Association

In the past decade, the Leadership Summit has become WCA's flagship event. WCA's other conferences eventually grew to more than fifty events per year, both on-site and via satellite.

Reinventing Willow Creek Association. In 2005, toward the end of the run of double-digit annual growth, Mellado noticed that the WCA team had become seduced by its own success. Some important organizational disciplines had begun to wane due to the thinking that they were immune from the need for organizational change. In a 2011 lecture to the New York City Leadership Center Fellows Class, Mellado said,

> Let me describe the 2006 to 2009 time frame. Trouble began to brew in 2006. By that time there were 450 teaching church conferences in the United States that were, in a sense, competing with WCA. Our team was exhausted from the breadth of what we were trying to do. Simply speaking, we were in over our heads. We had waded out too far and were being swept away by our own enthusiasm and sense of invulnerability.[9]

During this time, Mellado had a parallel personal experience. In July 2007, while vacationing with his family in Baja, California, Mellado and his thirteen-year-old son, Davy, went swimming. "We planned to play in the shallow water for a few minutes and then continue on our way. But as Davy and I started to bodysurf, the current pulled us deeper into the ocean."

In seconds, they were too far out to shout for help, and already Davy was struggling to stay afloat. In a moment of panic and terror, Mellado realized that they did not have the strength to swim to shore. He was certain they would die within minutes.

"I imagined my wife and daughter attending our double funeral and did not want that to be my final memory. In that moment I considered my own life expendable but not Davy's. I called upon reserves I did not know I had to get Davy back to shore."

Miraculously, Mellado was able to guide his son back to safety. He too survived, but barely. "The exertion and trauma caused my kidneys to shut down, and I suffered acute renal failure."

After multiple rounds of dialysis and a lengthy recovery, Mellado emerged from the ordeal. But the near-death experience changed him. "The startling reminder of the fragility of life made me more grateful for it and more determined to use it well."[10]

Surviving that experience gave Mellado the hope and confidence to believe that WCA could also survive.

So in 2009, Mellado, Bell and the rest of the executive team worked through another "reboot." Calling on reserves of strength they did not know they had, they focused on what was most important to save: the Leadership Summit. They greatly expanded it both domestically and internationally, and officially renamed it the Global Leadership Summit.

By 2009, international involvement more than doubled—from 24,000 to 54,000—and nearly tripled by 2010, reaching more than 65,000 registrants.

But then came another wave—the financial crash of 2008. In 2009, seventy staff members (fifty-six FTEs, i.e., full-time equivalents) were laid off. At the same time WCA shed a number of its ministry divisions and established the following priorities:

Double our efforts around what's working and most effective. Consequently, WCA focused on growing the Global Leadership Summit even more.

Change the economic model. WCA shifted from being 90 percent fee-for-service revenues to 70 percent fee-for-service dependent, and increased the funds raised from 10 to 30 percent. WCA has been effective in appealing for scholarship support of global leaders. In 2010, as a result of the freewill offering taken during the Global Leadership Summit, nearly 30 percent of the needed international budget was raised.

Cut costs. WCA became ruthlessly disciplined to return to financial health in a short period.[11]

According to Mellado and Bell, another essential organizational lesson learned during this difficult era was: *Do not forget about tomorrow.*

In 2009, Jim Collins published a book titled *How the Mighty Fall.* In it he writes about mature organizations that transition from the peak of their success to "denial of risk and peril to ultimately become irrelevant or dead."[12] The warning given by Collins was unfolding right before the eyes of WCA's leadership team. To survive, they would have to reinvent the organization while riding the waves of a wildly changing cultural and economic climate.

WCA was able to emerge from the crisis due to the talent of the leadership team—their confidence in one another and their passion for the vision enabled them to deploy resources to meet the challenges.

CONSEQUENTIAL IMPACT

Despite organizational and financial challenges, and its own near-death experiences, Willow Creek Association has given new life to churches around the world. In a 2007 survey of more than two thousand of the largest non-Catholic congregations in the nation, Willow Creek Community Church was ranked as the most influential church by Church Growth Today, due largely to the ongoing impact and ministry of WCA. Half of the churches in the top fifty were member churches of Willow Creek Association.[13] WCA has helped to create a culture of excellence and collegiality among churches.

In greater New York, the Leadership Summit was planted at the Presbyterian Church of New Providence in 2003. In 2005 the Leadership Summit was expanded to six new sites, including all five boroughs of New York City, Long Island and Connecticut.

Between 2005 and 2010, more than fifteen thousand leaders from metro New York participated in the Summit in fifty-six sites (aggregate numbers).

When the Leadership Summit began in the New York City area, some were concerned about whether a suburban church could design a conference for urban New Yorkers. Attendance at the first Summit dispelled that concern. Participation was 72 percent ethnic minority, predominantly Hispanic and African American. On a scale of one to ten, the attendees from minority backgrounds graded the experience a 9.5. The impact of the Leadership Summit was powerful for three primary reasons.

Access to world-class speakers and thinkers at an affordable cost. In New York City, two-thirds of the pastors have not finished seminary, and one-third have not finished college. Many leaders are bivocational, and they serve a Christian community that is more than 90 percent minority and international. Having access to world-class speakers and thinkers at an affordable cost is a huge benefit.

Large-scale leadership gathering. Large cities need large numbers of leaders who are learning and working together. Over the course of a two-day event, leaders get more time together than they do the rest of the year combined.

A global movement in a global city attracts global leaders. Meeting in a global city like New York, the Leadership Summit connects global leaders. Thousands of Hispanic, Caribbean and Asian New York leaders identify with and are connected to leaders in cities around the globe.

The Leadership Summit elevates the thinking of leadership teams and helps them visualize possibilities. The New York City Leadership Center was conceived in large part due to the influence of Willow Creek Association and the training provided by the Leadership Summit. Bill Hybels has spoken every year on the theme "leaders do what leadership requires."

The Global Leadership Summit is a place where leaders can bring their teams. WCA models what it preaches in the implementation of the Summit. A team is built to volunteer, to manage and to implement the largest leadership development conference in the history of the church.

The Global Leadership Summit provides two primary benefits to teams: (1) It infuses them with fresh ideas of what God wants them to consider; and (2) it introduces innovative leadership models.

The Global Leadership Summit has become a portal for best practices and big ideas. In 2010, Blake Myckoskie of Tom's Shoes talked about his model of compassion. For every pair of shoes sold, the company provides a pair of shoes for children in the Two-Thirds World. In 2009, Jessica Jackley, cofounder of Kiva, described the company's impact on thousands of poor people through its micro-lending initiative.

Reveal and engage. Willow Creek Association not only inspires leaders, but it also informs churches in best practices of spiritual formation. In 2004, Willow Creek Community Church took a survey to determine how people become Christ-centered. The results were so surprising that WCA adopted the survey, did additional research and widened the survey, and then began offering it to more churches. To date, more than fifteen hundred churches have participated, and more than 350,000 people have responded. The expanded survey, called REVEAL, was indeed a revelation, first to Bill Hybels and then to leaders across America.

The first "aha" of the research was that involvement in church activities was not positively or negatively correlated with evidence of spiritual growth. The only thing that was positively correlated to spiritual growth was the degree of relational intimacy with the person of Jesus Christ. Looking at spiritual development through this lens, four unique stages along a spiritual continuum emerged: (1) exploring Christ, (2) growing in Christ, (3) close to Christ, and (4) Christ-centered.

Conversion takes place between stage one and two. Spiritual practices develop between stages two and three, and sacrificial giving and service develop between stages three and four—all based on growing intimacy with Jesus.

The second "aha" of the study was the gap between stages three and four. In fact, the study revealed that moving from "close to Christ" to "Christ-centered" is the biggest challenge for a Christian to navigate.

During their May 2011 visit to New York City, Mellado and Bell mapped out the conclusions of their research and made the following recommendations for church leadership teams:

1. *Embed the Bible in everything.* Reflection on Scripture was in fact the most catalytic practice for spiritual growth across the entire spiritual continuum.

2. *Get people moving on a journey.* Have clear "next steps" for people to get moving on their journey.

3. *Create ownership.* Help people see themselves as the "church" versus seeing the church as something they attend.

4. *Pastor the community.* Help the congregation integrate into the most important things going on in the community and see that involvement as ministry.[14]

Team influence. To WCA leadership, team means everything. Their purpose is "to maximize the transformative power of the local church." Their vision is "that every local church would realize its full redemptive potential." Their mission is "to stir up, equip and unite Christian leaders to build transformation-minded churches that will redeem and restore our broken world for Christ."[15] And the mission is the boss. Everything else is secondary.

From my observation, Mellado and Bell live out the values that have guided their team over the past fifteen years:

Humility. Everyone on the team defers to one another. They celebrate one another's gifts and create opportunities for one another to succeed.

Authenticity. Leaders on the team are transparent with one another. Mellado, by telling about his struggle to overcome the emotional as well as physical effects of his near-death experience, demonstrates how lessons learned in times of weakness can be used to strengthen others.

Endurance. Working together for the long term is essential. Mellado has been president of WCA for the last nineteen years of its twenty-year existence. Hybels has been at the helm of the church for thirty-seven years. Bell has been on the team for fifteen years. As a member of the Church Relations Field Team, Dave Wright has served hundreds of local Summit sites for more than a decade.

Friendship. The team travels together extensively. Rarely will you find a group of leaders who enjoy one another more and spend more time laughing with one another.

Bill Hybels states consistently that because of its role in stewarding the gospel of Christ, "the local church is the hope of the world." With this in mind, WCA believes the place to begin is with a strong team of shepherds who can lead people to spiritual maturity.

The stronger the team, the stronger the church. The stronger the team of churches in a community, the greater the impact on the community. As one Staten Island leader said, "The unity of the church is the hope of the community."[16]

VISION

As the Willow Creek Association executive team prepares for the future, they have identified their priorities. At the top of the list is to engage the ten thousand non-English-speaking congregations in America. Thousands of foreign-language churches meet in the

United States but have no meaningful contact with English-speaking churches.

WCA envisions being able to "diffuse innovation" into the 300,000 congregations in the United States by reaching the 16 percent of pioneer and early-adopter leaders. The team is working on models of how leaders can better connect with one another between the Global Leadership Summit annual events.

Globally, the vision is to influence the five hundred most influential cities. WCA is already connected in eighty-two countries (including seventeen of the fifty most underresourced countries in the world). But as the world becomes increasingly urban, the WCA team is looking for partners in every nation who want to connect the body of Christ through "leadership development for the sake of spiritual transformation" targeted to the leadership core of local churches.[17]

Mellado's leadership through the recent crisis years has positioned Willow Creek Association to continue to flourish for the decade to come. The WCA team has practiced what it has preached under Mellado—it has adjusted with great agility to rapidly changing climate conditions.

LEADER APPLICATION

- What can you do with your team at work or church to create a culture of shared values and passion? How will you arrive at the place where "the mission is the boss"?

- What large goal can your team commit to that will attract additional like-minded talent?

A prayer . . .

Jesus,

Grow into our leadership a passion for our vision that is larger than our organizational title. May we have a deeply held sense of mission with everyone on our teams.

JIM MELLADO, STEVE BELL AND THE WILLOW CREEK ASSOCIATION: KEY EVENTS

1975	Bill Hybels plants Willow Creek Community Church
1989	Peter Drucker features Willow Creek Community Church in *Harvard Business Review*
1991	Mellado writes *Harvard Business Review* case study on WCCC
1993	Mellado becomes president of Willow Creek Association
1995	WCA launches the Leadership Summit
1998	Steve Bell joins Willow Creek Association executive team
2005	WCA launches the Summit at international sites; WCA launches seven-site model for greater New York
2009	The Global Leadership Summit attendance surpasses 100,000 registrants in one year

15

Conclusion

CONSEQUENTIAL LEADERSHIP

The Difference One Person Can Make

In May 2012 my wife, Marya, and I spent fourteen hours over two weekends watching *The War,* a PBS documentary about World War II by Ken Burns. Marya's dad was a cook stationed in London at the end of the war. Before coming home, he was involved in the grisly work of cleaning up some of the concentration camps in Germany. The carnage of the war is indescribable. One estimate puts the loss of life at forty-eight million, including twenty million Soviet citizens and ten million Chinese, in addition to the six million Jews who were slaughtered.[1]

As nightmarish as those numbers are, it could have been much worse if the United States had not entered the war. Because of its military strength and vision for a free world, the United States, along with its allies, turned the tide, and the war was won in both the European and Pacific theaters in 1945. Without American involvement, world history would have been dramatically different and far worse.

After watching the documentary, I began asking myself, *what made it possible for the United States to play such a decisive role?*

ONE LEADER, ONE LECTURE, ONE LOCATION

Many factors determined the character of the United States in 1941, but the most important factor, I believe, is the character of one leader who changed the course of our nation many years earlier. That leader was Abraham Lincoln.

Lincoln preserved the Union at a terrible cost, but he preserved it. His rise to the presidency was catapulted by one speech in one location. On February 27, 1860, Lincoln gave his "Cooper Union" speech in downtown Manhattan. In it, he declared his position against slavery and its expansion to new territories. The speech galvanized northern voters to support his candidacy, and Lincoln leveraged the influence of New York City to electrify the nation. He emerged from obscurity as a small-time lawyer in Springfield, Illinois, to lead the nation.[2]

On January 1, 1863, nearly three years after the speech, President Lincoln signed the Emancipation Proclamation. With the stroke of a pen, he freed a community of African slaves who had been in captivity on American soil for nearly three centuries.

The Cooper Union speech had changed the world.

Two years later, on April 14, 1865, Lincoln was assassinated. But in the five years since declaring his position against slavery, he accomplished two remarkable feats: he preserved the Union, and he freed hundreds of thousands of slaves.

Lincoln was so beloved that his body was taken by train on a funeral pageant. Millions of Americans came to see him as he lay in Washington, D.C., Baltimore, Harrisburg, Philadelphia, New York City, Albany, Buffalo, Cleveland, Columbus, Indianapolis, Chicago and finally Springfield. In New York City an estimated 500,000 people stood along the procession route.[3]

The inscription below his statue on the Lincoln Memorial reads:

In this temple, as in the hearts of the people for whom he saved the Union, the memory of Abraham Lincoln is enshrined forever.[4]

Lincoln's Cooper Union speech was a defining moment for Lincoln and for the nation. On the strength of that speech, Lincoln was able to preserve the nation, which set in motion the events that made it possible for the United States to provide leadership that helped win the Second World War.

DEFINING MOMENTS

We all have defining moments—an experience when we barely escape death, participate in an historic event or gain clarity in the stillness of a sleepless night. I've had two near-death experiences, both involving car accidents. At age fourteen, while riding a bike downhill, I was hit by a car traveling fifty miles an hour. I bounced off the roof of the car and landed on the asphalt. I spent the summer recovering from a leg injury.

At age seventeen, I fell asleep while driving home after a junior-senior prom. I awakened just in time to avoid going into the ditch. I jerked the steering wheel and turned the car around with two wheels off the ground. I landed in the other ditch, facing the opposite direction. By then, God had my full attention, and he used that accident—along with the reading of the New Testament, a demonic encounter and the influence of friends—to lead me to make a decision two months later to follow Christ.

Within one month of my conversion I invited all of the high school youth groups in my small town to meet together. I knew instinctively that the unity of God's people mattered. I was converted not only to Jesus but also to the unity of his church. This became the dominant theme of my life—throughout my senior year of high school, university training, thirteen years of campus ministry and nearly thirty years in New York City. Along the way, other defining moments have sharpened that calling.

Psalm 23. In 1998 I was in a class taught by Dr. John Pippo at Eastern Baptist Theological Seminary. In the first week, Dr. Pippo had us spend an hour a day for four days with Psalm 23. In each of the four days, God spoke powerfully and differently to me. I was so moved by the experience that I decided to translate Psalm 23 from

Hebrew into English. In doing so I discovered that David described God by using fourteen verbs that convey unending action. For example, Psalm 23:3, which says, "[the Lord] guides me in paths of righteousness for his name's sake" (NIV 1984), means that God never ceases to guide us, and he continually guides us in the direction that will honor him. This defining moment has helped me to interpret all that God has done in my life.

First, my fifty-year journey can be understood chronologically. For the first half of my life I lived in rural South Dakota, where I was shaped by my family and my educational experiences through college. The second half of my life has been spent in New York City, where I have lived out the family, work and spiritual values shaped during the first half of my life.

Second, my journey can be understood geographically and thematically. I spent seventeen years immersed in the university with InterVarsity. The second season of life took me into the unity of the church, building bridges across ethnic and denominational lines through united prayer. The third season of my life has brought me to a greater understanding of the city, including global cities.

Third, my journey can be understood racially. I grew up in a small, homogenous community of northern Europeans. As I mentioned in chapter ten, I grew up with prejudice against two groups—Native Americans and African Americans. My hometown was sixteen miles from an Indian reservation where the unemployment rate was 80 percent. The bank my family has owned since 1914 had mixed results with loans to Native Americans. And my mother's family lived in the South, where the sharp separation between black and white still existed.

In moving to New York City I was confronted by the need to understand my ethnic identity and all of its assumptions. Being embraced by an African American family, who invited my family to live with theirs, was a life-changing experience. Attending church every Sunday for twenty-five years with a group of people in which sixty languages were spoken enlarged my soul. Being able to see "God's New Society" at church and in my work expanded my vision. Living in a community of one hundred language groups stretched my thinking. God has guided me in all of this for my own formation into the image of Christ, the unity of the church and the impact of the gospel in cities of the world.

Landing in New York City was not an accident. Living in my neighborhood, working with churches and networking cities is not a coincidence. God has guided and is guiding me into paths of righteousness for his name's sake—despite my constant wanderings and uneven obedience.

Ephesians 2. While traveling in East Africa in 2002, I had another defining moment. Witnessing the devastation of HIV and AIDS changed me forever. Seeing women in their twenties dying of AIDS, looking like they were fifty, was heart-wrenching. Meeting a mother who had unknowingly contracted AIDS from her husband and passed it onto her nursing daughter was heartbreaking. I realized that children were being orphaned by the HIV/AIDS pandemic six thousand times a day. The knowledge that a child was being orphaned every fifteen seconds a day by HIV/AIDS was life-altering.

On the plane ride home I read these verses: "For it is by grace you have been saved, through faith—and this is not from yourselves, it is the gift of God—not by works, so that no one can boast. For we are God's handiwork, created in Christ Jesus to do good works, which God prepared in advance for us to do" (Ephesians 2:8-10).

Although God did not cause the AIDS pandemic, the health crisis is an opportunity for the church to do the "good works" that he has prepared us to do. What greater purpose could there be than to address that which is devastating more lives, more communities and more countries than any humanitarian crisis in history?

Despite the enormity of the need, God's people are making progress. A quiet army of faith-filled and humanitarian leaders are saving tens of thousands of lives. From presidents of nations to anonymous volunteers and sponsors, believers from all parts of the world are working together and are turning the tide.

Philippians 3 and the book of Acts. Another defining moment that sharpened my sense of calling happened on April 22, 2011. It was Good Friday, and I was reading Colossians and Philippians when I came to this statement: "Not that I have already obtained all this, or have already been made perfect, but I press on to take hold of that for which Christ Jesus took hold of me" (Philippians 3:12 NIV 1984).

Writing from a Roman prison cell near the end of his life, Paul declared his holy intention. He was going to take hold of that for which Christ took hold of him. This is the secret of becoming a consequential leader—having a full understanding of why Christ has taken hold of you.

Paul's life intersected the great global realities discussed in this book. He traveled only to influential cities on his three missionary journeys. He was committed to the poor in his benevolent work in Jerusalem. He was reaching and molding young leaders as evidenced in his letters to Timothy and Titus.

The book of Acts opens after two cataclysmic events: the crucifixion and resurrection of Jesus. The disciples were dazed and confused as to what was going on. Peter had denied the Lord. Thomas doubted the Lord. The women had been abandoned by the disciples. In the middle of these strained relational dynamics, Jesus told his disciples to wait in Jerusalem. Wait and pray.

While they waited and prayed, God sent the Holy Spirit with such power that pilgrims from fifteen countries who had gathered in Jerusalem for Pentecost heard the gospel in their own languages. That day, three thousand of them were converted.

Into this new community God sent Barnabas, a Levite. Barnabas is a New Testament paradigm for consequential leadership. Without Barnabas there would not have been a Paul.

Barnabas was philanthropic. We are introduced to Barnabas

after he sold property and gave it to the disciples to be distributed as needed (Acts 4). He understood that we need nothing else when we have God and each other. He put into practice his conviction that everything belongs to God.

Barnabas was a spiritual parent. After the conversion of Saul, Barnabas became his advocate and mentor. Before conversion, Saul was the most feared and violent anti-Christian in the first century, sending many believers to prison and death. The disciples would have nothing to do with him even after his conversion. But Barnabas began a mentoring relationship with him that lasted for decades and changed the world. When he started the relationship, he had no way of knowing that Saul, the killer of Christians, would become the apostle Paul, the most famous of all Christian missionaries.

Barnabas was generous toward the poor. After retrieving Paul from the desert, he took him to Jerusalem (Acts 11). They traveled four hundred miles on foot to deliver an offering to Jewish Christians. Ray Bakke believes that this was part of Paul's training—to take the hunger offering to the Jews before taking the gospel offering to the Gentiles.[5] Paul was being trained to understand the importance of the social and humanitarian dimension of the gospel.

Barnabas was a prayerful leader. Perhaps the most important prayer meeting in history took place when Barnabas was in Antioch with European, Asian, African and Jewish church leaders (Acts 13:1-3). In the context of this international community, God spoke to him and Paul about their mission assignment.

The second half of Acts reports how the gospel reached the major cities of Asia and Europe. The book ends with Paul in Rome fulfilling God's assignment to take the gospel to the Gentiles and their kings (Acts 9:15).

Barnabas was a peacemaker. Barnabas and Paul walked hundreds of miles to attend the Jerusalem Council (see Acts 15). This was a defining moment in spiritual history. They appealed to Jewish Christians to embrace God's work among the Gentiles. Within a few decades of the crucifixion, the gospel was planted in Asia, Europe and Africa. Paul later wrote: "Make every effort to keep the unity of the Spirit through the bond of peace" (Ephesians 4:3).

Divine guidance. Many people in my life have been like Barnabas to me—Ray Bakke, Billy Graham, John Perkins and John Stott, as well as the leaders I interviewed for this book. In addition, David Bryant, founder of Concerts of Prayer International, poured into my life for more than a decade, helping me to understand spiritual and cultural movements. Also, the pastors in metropolitan New York City, especially those who cross racial and denominational lines, have been influential.

In 2008, a significant event and an influential person intersected my life. I attended the Halftime Institute in Dallas as the guest of Bob Buford, a mentor for thousands of leaders worldwide. His book *Halftime* has sold more than half a million copies. The event came at a perfect time for me. My father had died the month before, and I felt disoriented. Also, after living in New York City for twenty-four years, I was starting the New York City Leadership Center and I wanted a stronger sense of where God was leading.

In addition to reading the book *Halftime,* we took the StrengthsFinder test. I discovered that my top three strengths were Learner, Achiever and Activator. We were asked to dream on paper and to map what we believed God wanted us to do over the next twenty years. I drew a picture of Manhattan with the Empire State Building adjacent to drawings of Europe, Asia and Africa. I believed that the New York City Leadership Center and its partners would attract leaders from around the world, train and equip them, encourage them, and send them off to do great collaborative work that demonstrates the love of Christ in their cities.

In the spring of 2011, I reviewed the map I had drawn in 2008. Taking into account the events that we hosted in 2010, including our major training at the Empire State Building and our Movement Day National Conference, I realized that the 2008 prediction had come ten years ahead of schedule. God was indeed guiding us into paths of righteousness for his name's sake. We had already hosted eight hundred leaders from thirty-four cities and fourteen nations. This exercise confirmed what I learned in my study of Psalm 23.

Relentlessly and unceasingly, God is using defining events and godly people to guide all of us in the way of righteousness. My own personal leadership lessons include:

- A guiding worldview is essential. Based on my worldview, I believe the following:
  1. Cities shape culture.
  2. Gospel movements change cities.
  3. Catalytic leaders launch movements.
  4. Mentors and catalytic events shape leaders.

- Choices matter. God has given us an incredible freedom to choose how we spend our lives.

Now consider the following questions as you examine God's leading in your own life:

- What three defining moments shaped you and caused you to become who you are?

- Who are your primary mentors? How have they influenced you? Whom are you mentoring? How?

- Where is God leading you? Where are you leading others?

- What catalytic event can you participate in to renew your vision and to inform your choices?

- Considering Barnabas, what areas of his leadership resonate with you, and what areas do you need to develop?

A prayer . . .

Jesus,

I pray that we may live our lives consequentially. Help us to be the kind of mentors and heroes who will give others the vision to become all that you intend them to be. Help us to craft experiences that point them toward the place you have set aside for them. Allow us to live our lives generously for the sake of others.

Afterword

The future of culture, the future of nations and the future of the church are in large part determined by the work of consequential leaders in every sector of society. There can be no less important subject to examine. The leaders profiled in this work are doing what many Christian leaders would have once thought impossible. The work of these leaders extends beyond the influencers in urban culture to the poorest of the poor around the world, vulnerable children and other people in need. Any leader looking to make a difference will benefit from these case studies.

I've known Mac for more than fifteen years. We've talked off and on about our dreams for seeing cities transformed, churches revived and unity among believers of all backgrounds. It's been a joy to reconnect with Mac over the last three years related to Movement Day, an effort to gather thousands of leaders who share a heart for seeing movements raised up in large cities around the world. I appreciate Mac's kingdom mindset, and the way he looks to build partnerships for the greater good. God has used his work with NYC Leadership Center to inspire many other cities and leaders to live out their calling and make a difference. Mac's own very consequential leadership in a number of different areas makes him the perfect person to author this book.

"Seeking the peace and prosperity" (Jeremiah 29:7) of the cities to which God has called us benefits the common good and advances the kingdom. It challenges Christ followers to move out of their Christian subculture and into the context in which God has placed them. As leaders serve others, we begin to see God's face in the "least of these" and watch as he moves powerfully to accomplish his purposes.

For leaders in any sector of society, this book has challenged us to greater things. Whether you are an entrepreneur, nonprofit leader, church planter, political leader, or simply a Christ follower and concerned citizen, you cannot overlook the importance of serving others, living out Christ's teachings and looking for the best ways to use your position of leadership for the greatest kingdom impact.

This book is a study of what has already taken place through several consequential leaders, but it is also a challenge to every Christ follower to continue and multiply that work. Having seen the momentum that is taking place in the body of Christ today, we cannot help but be confronted by what God may be asking of each of us in the movements he is leading.

Don't let your conviction stop with the reading of this book. Get connected with other leaders in your community and pray for the vision and resources to make these ideas a reality where you live. God will equip you and show you the way to become a consequential leader for his glory and the good of all.

We can do more together than we ever could alone. We have so much to learn from each other. And there is so much work yet to be done.

KEVIN PALAU
President, Luis Palau Association

Notes

Foreword

[1]Joseph A. Maciariello and Karen E. Linkletter, *Drucker's Lost Art of Management: Peter Drucker's Timeless Vision for Building Effective Organizations* (New York: McGraw-Hill, 2011).

[2]Peter Drucker, "Management's New Paradigms," *Forbes,* October 5, 1998.

Chapter 1: Introduction

[1]Ralph Winter, *Perspectives on the World Christian Movement* (Pasadena, Calif.: Paternoster, 1999), pp. 152-63.

[2]Ray Bakke, foreword to *The Power of a City at Prayer,* by Mac Pier and Katie Sweeting (Downers Grove, Ill.: InterVarsity Press, 2002), p. 9.

[3]Ray Bakke, personal interview, September 30, 2010.

[4]Ibid.

[5]Lauren E. Glaze, "Correctional Populations in the United States, 2009 Bureau of Justice Statistics Bulletin," December 2010 <http://bjs.ojp .usdoj.gov/content/pub/pdf/cpus09.pdf>.

[6]Ibid.

[7]Gary Frost, personal interview, November 19, 2007.

[8]Tony Dungy, television interview by Bob Costas, NBC Sports, January 10, 2009.

[9]Associated Press, "Indianapolis Among School District with Lowest Graduation Rate," WNDU.com, April 1, 2008 <www.wndu.com/education/ headlines/17184036.html>.

[10]Mac Pier, "11355: The Soul of Flushing," research paper for a course on community transformation at Eastern Baptist Theological Seminary, August 1998.

[11]Doug Seebeck, personal interview, July 18, 2011.

Chapter 2: Tim Keller

[1]Timothy Keller, interview by Mac Pier, March 7, 2011.

[2]Timothy Keller, *King's Cross: The Story of the World in the Life of Jesus* (New York: Dutton, 2011), p. xvi.

[3]Keller interview.

[4]Mac Pier, *Spiritual Leadership in the Global City* (Birmingham, Ala.: New Hope Publishers, 2008), p. 141.

[5]Keller interview.

[6]Timothy Keller, *Redeemer City to City Year End Report,* December 2010.

[7]The Church Report, "50 Most Influential Churches," *Christianity Today,* July 2006.

[8]George W. Bush, *Decision Points* (New York: Crown Publishing, 2010), p. 33.

[9]The New York City Movement Project is an effort to change New York City through church planting and leader development. It is also designed to accelerate gospel movements in large U.S. cities.

[10]Conference call with Tim Keller, Bob Doll and Katherine Barnhart, November 3, 2011.

[11]Keller interview.

[12]Ibid.

[13]Timothy Keller, address to New York City pastors, Redeemer Presbyterian Church Offices, May 2009; Timothy Keller, *The Prodigal God* (New York: Dutton, 2008).

[14]Keller, *Prodigal God,* p. 11.

[15]Timothy Keller, "Why We Need to Reach Cities" (address, Cape Town 2010, Cape Town, South Africa, October 2010).

[16]Tony Carnes, Values Research Institute, September 15, 2009.

[17]Tim Keller, Movement Day Conference, September 30, 2010, New York City.

[18]"It Started with One," North American Mission Board, September 2007.

[19]Keller interview.

[20]Ibid.

[21]Pier, *Spiritual Leadership,* p. 33.

Chapter 3: Luis Palau

[1]Ethan Cole, "Luis Palau Preaches to Thousands in Communist Vietnam," *The Christian Post,* April 11, 2011 <www.christianpost.com/news/luis-palau-preaches-to-thousands-in-communist-vietnam-49793/>.

[2]Hongnak Koo, *The Impact of Luis Palau on Global Evangelization* (Grand Rapids: Credo Publishing, 2010), p. 37.

[3]Luis Palau and Kevin Palau, interview with Mac Pier, June 2, 2011.

[4]Koo, *Impact of Luis Palau,* pp. 36-37.

[5]Terry Whalin, *Luis Palau* (Minneapolis: Bethany, 1996), pp. 26-31.

[6]Koo, *Impact of Luis Palau,* p. 50.

[7]Ibid., p. 38.

[8]Ibid., pp. 50-51.

[9]Ibid., pp. 269-71.

[10]Palau interview.

[11]Koo, *Impact of Luis Palau,* pp. 50-52.

[12]Palau interview.

[13]Koo, *Impact of Luis Palau,* p. 57.

[14]Palau interview.

[15]Ibid.

[16]Koo, *Impact of Luis Palau,* pp. 13-14.

[17]Richard N. Ostling, "The Battle for Latin America's Soul," *Time,* June 24, 2001, p. 2.

[18]John L. Allen Jr., "The Dramatic Growth of Evangelicals in Latin America," *National Catholic Reporter,* August 18, 2006, pp. 1-2.

[19]Jose Orozco, "Latin America: Evangelical Christianity Moves the Masses— A Report from Venezuela," *Religio Scope,* December 8, 2004, pp. 1-2.

[20]Michelle A. Vu, "Luis Palau, Rescued Miner Speak of Hope in Christ at Chile Festival," *The Christian Post,* November 3, 2010, p. 1.

[21]Koo, *Impact of Luis Palau,* p. 230.

[22]Ibid., p. 225.

[23]Ibid., p. 231.

[24]Ibid., p. 237.

[25]Tom Krattenmaker, "Evangelism 2.0," *USA Today,* July 20, 2009.

[26]Rusty Wright, "Evangelism: Downtown Evangelism Makes a Comeback," *Christianity Today,* January 8, 2001.

[27]Palau interview.

Chapter 4: A. R. Bernard

[1]Bakke has traveled to 250 cities with a population of a million or more.

[2]A. R. Bernard Sr., "Former Black Muslim Speaks About Hope in Jesus," interviewed on *The 700 Club,* CBN <www.cbn.com/700club/guests/bios/ AR_Bernard_072104.aspx>.

[3]Mac Pier, *Spiritual Leadership in the Global City* (Birmingham, Ala.: New Hope Publishing, 2008), pp. 203-4.

[4]Bernard and Karen were high school sweethearts. They married at age 19.

[5]Pier, *Spiritual Leadership,* pp. 203-4.

[6]Ibid., p. 204.

[7]Ibid., p. 54.

[8]N. R. Kleinfield, "Big Pulpit," *The New York Times,* May 21, 2009.

[9]A. R. Bernard, interview by Mac Pier, July 7, 2011.

[10]"About Us," Christian Cultural Center website <www.cccinfo.org/ aboutus>.

[11]Ibid.

[12]See The Council of Churches of the City of New York website <www.cccny .net/history.html>.

[13]Estimates in 2011 are that 17 percent of New York City residents have an evangelical faith. Tony Carnes, Values Research Institute, 2010 study.

[14]Bernard interview.

[15]Ibid.

[16]Ibid.

Chapter 5: Glenn Smith

[1]Glenn Smith, "Community Development in Canada," *Christian Direction,* Quebec, 2008.

[2]Lausanne was started in 1974 when Billy Graham convened Christian leaders from every nation in Lausanne, Switzerland. The vision of Lausanne is to track and accelerate the growth of Christianity around the globe.

[3]Glenn Smith, interview by Mac Pier, October 20, 2010.

[4]Ibid.

[5]Ibid.

[6]Smith, "Community Development," p. 21.

[7]Ibid., p. 16.

[8]Smith interview.

[9]Glenn Smith, "Urban Mission Methodology: The Challenges of Urban Mission," *Lausanne World Pulse,* September 2006, pp. 18-23.

[10]Glenn Smith, "Key Indicators of a Transformed City," *Christian Direction,* Quebec, 2008, pp. 2-3.

[11]Ibid., p. 16.

[12]See the Christian Direction website at <www.direction.ca> for a more complete list of agencies that Christian Direction has partnered with.

[13]Canadian philosopher Charles Taylor gives this explanation of the term *social imaginary:* "the ways in which [people] imagine their social existence, how they fit together with others, how things go on between them and their fellows, the expectations which are normally met, and the deeper normative notions and images which underlie these expectations." Charles Taylor, *Modern Social Imaginaries* (Durham, N.C.: Duke University Press, 2004), pp. 23, 115. In his magnum opus, *A Secular Age* (Cambridge, Mass.: The Belknap Press of Harvard University, 2007), Taylor further develops these concepts in chapter four.

[14]Smith, "Urban Mission Methodology," pp. 9-10.

[15]Smith, "Key Indicators," pp. 10-11.

[16]Smith interview.

Chapter 6: Richard Stearns

[1]Richard Stearns, *The Hole in Our Gospel: What Does God Expect of Us?* (Nashville: Nelson, 2009), pp. 82-84.

[2]John Ortberg, *If You Want to Walk on Water, You've Got to Get Out of the Boat* (Grand Rapids: Zondervan, 2001). Quoted in Stearns, *Hole in Our Gospel,* p. 93.

[3]Stearns, *Hole in our Gospel,* p. 31.

[4]Ibid., p. 25.

[5]Richard Stearns et al., *Nonprofit Leadership in a For-Profit World: Essential Insights from 15 Christian Executives* (Cincinnati, Ohio: Standard, 2011), p. 202.

[6]Richard Stearns, interview by Mac Pier, June 13, 2011.

[7]Stearns interview. According to Stearns, "The work of Concerts of Prayer and the New York City Leadership Center was an important partner to help World Vision establish itself with the church community in New York City."

[8]Ibid.

[9]Princess Zulu, United Nations World Vision Women's Event, September 2004.

[10]Stearns, *Hole in Our Gospel*, p. 7.

[11]Ibid., p. 194.

[12]Ibid., p. 10.

[13]Richard Stearns, "Cast and Live Your Vision," *Outcomes Magazine,* Fall 2010.

[14]Stearns, *Hole in Our Gospel,* pp. 147-48.

[15]Stearns interview.

[16]The cost to provide needed medicine had declined from $12,000 per year to $300 due to the availability of drugs because of the PEPFAR grant from the United States.

[17]George W. Bush, *Decision Points* (New York: Crown Publishing, 2010), pp. 337-39.

[18]World Vision International, *HIV and AIDS Initiative,* 2005.

[19]Stearns interview.

[20]World Vision Annual Reports 1998-2010.

[21]<www.worldvision.org/content.nsf/about/why-donate>.

[22]Stearns interview.

[23]Ibid.

[24]Ibid.

[25]Ibid.

Chapter 7: Ajith Fernando

[1]Ajith Fernando, "Bible Exposition: Ephesians" (address, Cape Town 2010 video, October 19, 2010) <http://conversation.lausanne.org/en/conversations/detail/11327>.

[2]American Express has employee networks that "bring people of similar backgrounds and interests together." Among them are SALT (the Christian network), CHAI (the Jewish network) and PEACE (the Muslim network). "Common backgrounds, uncommon passion" <http://careers.american express.com/working/diversity/employee-networks.html>.

[3]British Prime Minister Winston Churchill described the moment a Japanese fleet prepared to invade Sri Lanka as "the most dangerous and distressing moment of the entire conflict." Commonwealth Air Training Program Museum, "The Saviour of Ceylon" <www.airmuseum.ca/mag/0410.html>.

[4]"Sri Lanka Leader Hails 'Victory,'" BBC News, May 19, 2009 <http://news.bbc.co.uk/2/hi/south_asia/8056752.stm>.

[5]"Buddhism in South Asia," Buddhist World, 2008 <http://www.buddhanet.net/e-learning/buddhistworld/south-asia.htm>.

[6]Central Intelligence Agency, *The World Factbook: Sri Lanka* <https://www.cia.gov/library/publications/the-world-factbook/geos/ce.html>.

[7]Michael Hardy, "Poverty in Sri Lanka," *The Sunday Leader,* April 4, 2010 <www.thesundayleader.lk/2010/04/04/poverty-in-sri-lanka/>.

[8]Ajith Fernando, interview by Mac Pier, May 30, 2010.

[9]Priyan Fernando, interview by Mac Pier, August 18, 2011.

[10]Ajith Fernando interview.

[11]Ibid.

[12]Ajith Fernando, *The Call to Joy and Pain* (Wheaton, Ill.: Crossway, 2007), p. 52.

[13]Ajith Fernando interview.

[14]Fernando, *Call to Joy and Pain*, p. 53.

[15]"Up to 100,000 Killed in Sri Lanka's Civil War: UN," ABC News Australia, May 21, 2009 <www.abc.net.au/news/stories/2009/05/20/2576543.htm>.

[16]Ajith Fernando interview.

[17]Ibid.

[18]Fernando, *Call to Joy and Pain,* p. 9.

[19]Ajith Fernando interview.

[20]Fernando, *Call to Joy and Pain,* pp. 37, 39.

[21]Rodney Stark, *The Rise of Christianity: How the Obscure, Marginal Jesus Movement Became the Dominant Religious Force in the Western World in a Few Centuries* (San Francisco: HarperSanFrancisco, 1997), pp. 73-94.

[22]Fernando, *Call to Joy and Pain,* p. 86.

[23]Ajith Fernando interview.

[24]Fernando, *Call to Joy and Pain,* p. 76.

[25]Ajith Fernando interview.

[26]Ibid.

[27]Ajith Fernando, *Jesus Driven Ministry* (Wheaton, Ill.: Crossway, 2002), pp. 13-14.

[28]Ibid., p. 14.

[29]Ajith Fernando interview.

[30]Fernando, *Jesus Driven Ministry,* p. 23.

Chapter 8: Frances Hesselbein

[1]Frances Hesselbein, curriculum vitae, The Frances Hesselbein Leadership Institute <www.hesselbeininstitute.org/about/fhbio.html>.

[2]Frances Hesselbein, *My Life in Leadership* (San Francisco: Jossey-Bass, 2011), p. 154.

[3]Debbe Kennedy, "3 Leadership Lessons for Women," Global Dialogue Center, May 20, 2009.

[4]Hesselbein, *Life in Leadership*, p. 4.

[5]Frances Hesselbein, interview by Mac Pier, May 31, 2011.

[6]Hesselbein, *Life in Leadership*, p. 5.

[7]Hesselbein interview.

[8]Hesselbein, *Life in Leadership*, pp. 52-53.

[9]Ibid., pp. 54-55.

[10]Hesselbein interview.

[11]Hesselbein, *Life in Leadership*, p. 73.

[12]Hesselbein interview.

[13]Ibid.

[14]Hesselbein, *Life in Leadership*, pp. 173-74.

[15]Hesselbein interview.

[16]Arati Menon Caroll, "Corporate Dossier," *The Economic Times*, January 15, 2010.

[17]Joanne Fritz, "Frances Hesselbein's 'Life in Leadership': A Review," December 28, 2010 <http://nonprofit.about.com/od/general/fr/Frances-Hesselbeins-Life-In-Leadership-A-Review.htm>.

[18]Hesselbein, *Life in Leadership*, p. 208.

[19]Cindy Gill, "To Serve Is to Live," *Pitt Magazine*, Winter 2010 <www.pittmag.pitt.edu/?p=1812>.

[20]Hesselbein interview.

[21]Ibid.

[22]Ibid.

[23]John Byrne, "Profiting from the Nonprofits," *Business Week*, March 25, 1990, p. 72.

[24]Hesselbein interview.

[25]Ibid.

[26]Frances Hesselbein, "Farewell to Chair" (farewell speech given at West Point, New York, April 28, 2011).

[27]Hesselbein interview.

[28]Ibid.

[29]Ibid.

[30]Ibid.

[31]Ibid.

[32]Fritz, "Frances Hesselbein."

Chapter 9: W. Wilson Goode Sr.

[1]Wilson Goode, interview by Mac Pier, May 23, 2011.

[2]The photo appears in Goode's autobiography, W. Wilson Goode with Joann Stevens, *In Goode Faith* (Valley Forge, Penn.: Judson Press, 1992), p. 188.

[3]Goode interview.

[4]Ibid.

[5]Amy S. Rosenberg, "Wilson Goode Finds Peace in the Pulpit," *Philadelphia Inquirer,* January 17, 2011, p. 5.

[6]Goode, *In Goode Faith,* p. 34.

[7]Rosenberg, "Peace in the Pulpit," p. 4.

[8]Goode, *In Goode Faith,* pp. 170-72.

[9]Ibid., p. 180.

[10]Ibid., p. 186.

[11]Rosenberg, "Peace in the Pulpit."

[12]Goode interview.

[13]Rosenberg, "Peace in the Pulpit," p. 5.

[14]Ibid.

[15]"States and Black Incarceration in America," *Mother Jones Magazine* <www.gibbsmagazine.com/blacks_in_prisons.htm>.

[16]Michelle Alexander, "The New Jim Crow," *Huffpost Books*, February 8, 2010 <www.huffingtonpost.com/michelle-alexander/the-new-jim-crow_b_454469.html>.

[17]Lauren E. Glaze, "Correctional Populations in the United States, 2009" *Bureau of Justice Statistics* (December 2010) <http://bjs.ojp.usdoj.gov/content/pub/pdf/cpus09.pdf>.

[18]The Pew Center on the States, "One in 100: Behind Bars in America 2008," *The Pew Charitable Trusts* (February 2008) <www.pewcenteronthestates.org/uploadedFiles/8015PCTS_Prison08_FINAL_2-1-1_FORWEB.pdf>.

[19]Rosenberg, "Peace in the Pulpit," p. 7.

[20]Ibid., p. 9.

[21]Wilson Goode, "Mentoring Children of Incarcerated Parents," Amachi, December 15, 2007 <www.youtube.com/watch?v=clYS9x6yc_g>.

[22]Goode interview.

[23]Rosenberg, "Peace in the Pulpit," pp. 3-4.

[24]Goode interview.

[25]Rosenberg, "Peace in the Pulpit," p. 10.

[26]Goode interview.

[27]Ibid.

Chapter 10: George Gallup Jr.

[1]Sarah Van Allen, "Corporate History," Gallup website <www.gallup.com/corporate/1357/corporate-history.aspx#2>.

[2]George Gallup Jr. with William Proctor, *Forecast 2000* (New York: Morrow, 1984), pp. 7, 21.

[3]Van Allen, "Corporate History."

[4]George Gallup Jr., interview with Mac Pier, May 26, 2011.

[5]Christian Union, *Under God's Power: Princeton Alumni and the Pursuit of Faith* (Princeton, N.J.: Christian Union, 2009), pp. 30-31.

[6]Ibid.

[7]James D. Davis, "World Evangelists Gather for Amsterdam Conference," *Sun Sentinel,* July 7, 1986.

[8]Gallup interview.

[9]Gallup interview.

[10]George H. Gallup International Institute, *Youthviews: The Newsletter of the Gallup Youth Survey,* Princeton, New Jersey.

[11]George Gallup Jr. with D. Michael Lindsay, *Surveying the Religious Landscape* (Harrisburg, Penn.: Morehouse, 2000), p. 40.

[12]Gallup interview.

Chapter 11: Brenda Salter McNeil

[1]Brenda Salter McNeil and Rick Richardson, *The Heart of Racial Justice* (Downers Grove, Ill.: InterVarsity Press, 2004), pp. 59-60.

[2]Brenda Salter McNeil, interview by Mac Pier, May 31, 2011.

[3]Ibid.

[4]Ibid.

[5]Ibid.

[6]Brenda Salter McNeil, "Behold, the Global Church," *Christianity Today,* November 17, 2006 <www.christianitytoday.com/ct/2006/november/34.42.html>.

[7]McNeil, "Behold, Global Church."

[8]Ibid.

[9]Ibid.

[10]McNeil and Richardson, *Heart of Racial Justice,* p. 99.

[11]Ibid., p. 102.

[12]McNeil, "Behold, Global Church."

[13]McNeil and Richardson, *Heart of Racial Justice,* p. 39.

[14]Brenda Salter McNeil, "Courageous Leadership for Catalytic Times," Global Leadership Summit, Willow Creek Association, August 11, 2011.

[15]Paula Harris and Doug Schaupp, *Being White: Finding Our Place in a Multiethnic World* (Downers Grove, Ill.: InterVarsity Press, 2004).

[16]McNeil and Richardson, *Heart of Racial Justice*, p. 61.
[17]Adapted from ibid.
[18]McNeil interview.

Chapter 12: Alan and Katherine Barnhart

[1]Katherine and Alan Barnhart, interview by Mac Pier, August 28-29, 2011.
[2]Nicholas Barnhart, interview by Mac Pier, August 29, 2011.
[3]Alan and Katherine Barnhart interview.
[4]Ibid.
[5]Alan Barnhart, "Profit with a Purpose" (National Christian Foundation, 2011), p. 24 <www.nationalchristian.com/download/474>.
[6]The Grove Group, "Policy, Guidelines, and Resources," Edition 2011.
[7]Joye Allen, interview by Mac Pier, August 29, 2011.
[8]Ibid.
[9]Alan and Katherine Barnhart interview.
[10]Ibid.
[11]Joye Allen interview.
[12]Alan and Katherine Barnhart interview.

Chapter 13: Bob Doll

[1]Bob Doll, "Global Economic Trends and Implications for the Global Church" (seminar at Cape Town 2010, Cape Town, South Africa, October 19, 2010).
[2]Halftime was started by Bob Buford, founder of Leadership Network, whose book *Halftime* (Grand Rapids: Zondervan, 1994) has sold more than 500,000 copies.
[3]Bob Doll, interview by Mac Pier, May 26, 2011.
[4]Ibid.
[5]Ibid.
[6]Ibid.
[7]Priyan Fernando, interview by Mac Pier, August 18, 2011.
[8]Bob Doll, "Our Story of Victory in Him" (2011 Christian Business Men's Connection Conference: Return to the Battlefield, Gettysburg, Penn., January 27-29, 2011) <www.cbmc.com/2011mensconference>.
[9]Bob Doll, interview with David Miller, Greenwich Leadership Forum, March 3, 2011.
[10]"Remarkable New Chapel Receives $1 Million Gift from the Dolls," Princeton HealthCare System Foundation <www.princetonhcs.org/page6477.aspx>.
[11]Ibid.
[12]Bob Doll interview with Mac Pier.
[13]Leslie Doll, interview by Mac Pier, August 14, 2011.

[14]Doug Birdsall, "Summary Report on Boston 2011 Biennial Meeting," Boston, August 2, 2011.

[15]Bob Doll interview with Mac Pier.

[16]Birdsall, "Summary Report."

[17]A tipping point happens when 10 percent of a community is energized to advance a particular conviction.

[18]Leslie Doll interview.

[19]Bob Doll, "Vision for a Gospel Movement" (presentation at Park Cities Baptist Church, Dallas, Tex., August 13, 2011).

[20]Doll interview with Mac Pier.

Chapter 14: Jim Mellado and Steve Bell

[1]Jim Mellado and Steve Bell, interview by Mac Pier, May 11, 2011.

[2]Ibid.

[3]"Willow History," Willow Creek Community Church website <www .willowcreek.org/aboutwillow/willow-history>.

[4]Jim Mellado, "Willow Creek Community Church," *Harvard Business Review,* February 23, 1999, p. 1.

[5]Peter Drucker, "What Business Can Learn from Non-Profits," *Harvard Business Review,* July-August 1989.

[6]Jim Mellado, "The Urgent Need for More and Better Leaders" (lecture to New York City pastoral leadership, Bowery Mission House, New York, New York, April 2005).

[7]Mellado and Bell interview.

[8]Gary Schwammlein, Biography, Willow Creek Association <www.spoke .com/info/p5DjJGt/GarySchwammlein>.

[9]Jim Mellado, "Leadership Lessons in Navigating Organizational Change" (lecture to the New York City Leadership Fellows Class, Fifth Avenue Presbyterian Church, New York, May 10, 2011).

[10]Jim Mellado, *Defining Moments Process Tool,* Willow Creek Association, 2008, pp. 1-2. Read the full account on the Willow Creek website: <www.willowcreek.no/willowcreek/vedlegg/450808%20Defining%20 Moments%20Process%20Tool.pdf>.

[11]Mellado, lecture to New York City Leadership Fellows Class.

[12]Jim Collins, *How the Mighty Fall* (New York: HarperCollins, 2009), p. 65.

[13]"Willow Creek Community Church Rated Most Influential in U.S.," *The Legal Record,* July 25, 2007.

[14]Steve Bell, "Engage: Learning from the Reveal Research" (lecture at Calvary Assembly of God, Staten Island, New York, May 10-12, 2011).

[15]Mellado and Bell interview.

[16]Lester Figueroa, Calvary Assembly of God, Staten Island, New York,

May 10, 2011.

[17]Mellado and Bell interview.

Chapter 15: Conclusion

[1]"Estimated War Dead: World War II," War Chronicle website, May 24, 2009 <http://warchronicle.com/numbers/WWII/deaths.htm>.

[2]Abraham Lincoln, "Cooper Union Address," Abraham Lincoln Online, Speeches and Writings, February 27, 1860, New York <http://showcase.netins.net/web/creative/lincoln/speeches/cooper.htm>.

[3]James Swenson, *Bloody Crimes: The Chase for Jefferson Davis & The Death Pageant for Lincoln's Corpse* (New York: HarperCollins, 2010), pp. 231, 275.

[4]"Lincoln Memorial," National Park Service website <www.nps.gov/nr/travel/presidents/lincoln_memorial.html>.

[5]Ray Bakke, lecture in New York.

Image Credits

Chapter 2: The Tim Keller photo was taken by Nathan Troester and is used courtesy of Redeemer Presbyterian Church.

Chapter 3: The Luis Palau photo is used courtesy of Benjamin Edwards Photography. ©Luis Palau Association.

Chapter 4: The A. R. Bernard photo was taken by and is used courtesy of Keith Major.

Chapter 5: The Glenn Smith photo is used courtesy of Christian Direction Inc. ©Christian Direction.

Chapter 6: The Richard Stearns photo was taken by Jon Warren and is used courtesy of World Vision. ©World Vision.

Chapter 7: The Ajith Fernando photo was taken by and is used courtesy of Asiri Fernando.

Chapter 8: The Frances Hesselbein photo is used courtesy of Frances Hesselbein Leadership Institute. ©Frances Hesselbein Leadership Institute.

Chapter 9: The W. Wilson Goode Sr. photo was taken by Christopher Capozziello and is used courtesy of Concerts of Prayer Greater New York.

Chapter 11: The Brenda Salter McNeil photo was taken by Victor Powell of Victor Powell Photography, and is used courtesy of Brenda Salter McNeil. ©Salter McNeil Associates.

Chapter 12: The Alan and Katherine Barnhart photo is used courtesy of the Barnhart family.

Chapter 13: The Bob Doll photo is used courtesy of BlackRock.

Chapter 14: The Jim Mellado photo is used courtesy of Corry Wiens/ Willow Creek Community Church.
   The Steve Bell photo was taken by Larry Dahlenburg and is used courtesy of the Willow Creek Association. ©Willow Creek Association.